After the Afterlife:
Memories of My Past Lives

Kelvin H. Chin

After the Afterlife:
Memories of My Past Lives
Kelvin H. Chin
Copyright © 2023 Kelvin H. Chin

For permission requests, please contact the author at
www.KelvinChin.org

Published in the United States by Aurelian Press.

ISBN 978-0-9977174-4-0

Jacket design: Sam "Wilhelmine" Chin
Book Cover Photo by Mario La Pergola on Unsplash
Interior design: Michael Grossman

With Affection...

to Jesse and Sam, my special children,
who I'm so happy found me once again,

to George, my ancient friend and brother,

to Widge, for his eye-opening letter,

to my closest friends and family who honored my request
to keep my memories to themselves for decades,

to my students worldwide who provide me with
new classrooms for my self-learning,

to my family and friends on the Other Side, especially my
former troops, who provide continual support for my efforts,

thank you all for nurturing and guiding me especially this
lifetime, this book honors you and our enduring friendships.

I have come to a place
where I am comfortable with the great unknown,
with not knowing everything,
with uncertainty,

Yet
with my emotional need to understand
still burning passionately within
as the fuel that has brought me
to the place where I am now,

Here
is a window into that journey…

Contents

Chapter 1

Reaching Back 6,000 Years

For the past 45 years, my past life memories have been resurfacing in my conscious awareness. So far, they reach back about 6,000 years, and they are drawn from about two dozen different lifetimes. I may have had many more lifetimes than two dozen over that span of time, however, so far I have varying degrees of memories from those two dozen.

I've never had a past life regression session. In fact, I did not even believe in reincarnation when my memories first spontaneously started resurfacing.

The only so-called "spiritual" practice I engaged in was learning to meditate when I was 19 years old at Dartmouth College. I learned Transcendental Meditation™ (TM) merely to help me reduce the intense anxiety I had at the time in college. That said, my involvement with meditation, and later becoming a TM teacher working closely with its founder, Maharishi Mahesh Yogi, was significant in the unfolding of my past lives.

My First Past Life Memory

In early 1977 I had a dream. It was an unusually powerful and intense emotional dream. Not the usual fantasy dreams I was used to having where a horse might sometimes change into a car, or where I was with different people doing different things in scenes that sometimes made sense, and other times did not. This dream was different.

In this dream I was all alone.

And the sadness was overwhelming. It left a mark in my consciousness. It turns out, I would remember it forever. However at the time I had it, I just chalked it up to some major "unstressing and releasing" of some old emotional baggage that night.

Fast forward six months or so, and I was on another advanced TM teacher meditation retreat in Switzerland. It was November 1977.

Every day everyone in our hotel convened in the morning and late afternoon for a "group program." We gathered in the hotel dining room where they had cleared out all the furniture, and replaced it with four-inch-thick twin-size foam mattresses.

One morning in the group meditation program, I involuntarily flipped over onto my back. The energy was so powerful that it "pushed me," so to speak, onto my back and my feet were up in the air — akin to a yoga pose called the "shoulder stand."

At the same time, my mind was filled with anguish, and the experience of physical pain, excruciating physical pain. Pain like I had never experienced before in my 20th century lifetime.

After a couple of weeks of this experience every time we meditated, my friend George Hammond and I went for our afternoon "walk and talk" after lunch. So on a beautiful afternoon in Wilderswil, he and I walked up a steep dirt path behind the hotel through a classic "picture postcard" Swiss pastoral hillside setting.

Then, I began to tell George about the dream I had earlier that year. I said something like, "George, I gotta tell you about this really powerful dream I had about 6-7 months ago…." Before I could get past that one sentence, he interrupted me and finished describing the dream!

I was shocked.

He described how dirty I was, covered with sand and grime, with dirt and sand around my face and in my mouth, tears streaked across my face, lying in a ditch along the side of a dirt road — emotionally distraught.

I said, "How did you know all that?"

George said, "Because I found you there. I was the one who found you. You don't know who you are?"

More on this later.

The Slave

After that first past life memory opened up in Switzerland, the next one started entering my awareness first during my meditations, then in the rest period after my meditations, and later simply during quiet moments while I was awake.

The initial image that appeared emblazoned in my mind was seeing myself from above floating on a piece of wreckage on what appeared to me to be the ocean. At least I thought it was the ocean because I could not see land from where I was.

I could see my half naked body from the back clinging to some wooden boards — what appeared to be a section of what used to be a larger structure — my "raft-like" cluster of boards being about 5 feet x 8 feet.

I had very dark black skin and I was roasting in the hot sun — feeling like I was being "roasted alive." Literally, I could feel the heat and the physical pain, or at least the memory of it.

Later experiences filled in more of this memory. And I could "taste" the very salty water, physically feel how parched my throat and mouth were, and even more clearly how painful the searing heat of the sun was on my body. I had only the rags of a loincloth covering me, with no protection from the direct sunlight.

I was quite literally clinging for dear life on a section of wood in the middle of a huge body of water.

At this point in my memories, I had no idea when or where or why I was having this experience. I only knew that it was a powerful experience that seemed "real," although my skeptical side continually questioned whether I was just making it all up in my imagination.

The fact that several months earlier I had a certain degree of "outside confirmation" from my friend George about my first seemingly past life memory did not fully make me a believer in reincarnation. I was still very skeptical of the whole notion of past lives and questioned these experiences, even though they were very powerful and seemed like recollections of events that were real.

Reincarnation simply was not part of my belief system growing up, and I had scoffed at it when I had heard other TM teachers openly discussing it on courses. I would roll my eyes and chuckle. I even made some derisive comments in private with my close meditator friends who also were non-believers in reincarnation.

After all, we were teaching meditation from the "science, education, sports and business" arm of the TM organization

— not with those flaky spiritual teachers from the "woo-woo" arm of the organization. We kept our distance from them, did not associate or even talk with them. We were in a completely separate part of the organization called the International Meditation Society (IMS) and the Students International Meditation Society (SIMS). Those SRM (Spiritual Regeneration Movement) teachers were "off the deep end" in our opinion!

But, over the next several weeks and months, I had more and more visions and data points that appeared in my consciousness about this memory of being on that wreckage. I saw myself chained down in a ship with many other men seated in rows on benches, with several of us on each oar. At some point, our ship exploded or was rammed — perhaps both — in a violent naval battle. And I ended up clinging to a large piece of a ship in what I later figured out was probably the Mediterranean Sea. That could explain my memory of the water tasting so very salty, since the Mediterranean is actually saltier than the open ocean, being an almost enclosed body of seawater. As such, I have since learned that over time and in certain seasons, the water evaporates leaving an even saltier sea.

The structure of the ships also explained the time period. It was ancient. And given that I was a very dark black-skinned African looking man, I was most likely enslaved by the Carthaginians who for hundreds of years were the rulers of the shipping lanes throughout the Mediterranean.

Before the Roman Empire finally defeated the Carthaginians in the last of the three Punic Wars, the two empires engaged in bloody naval and land battles for over 100 years from 264 to 146 B.C.

So, my best guess is that I was a Carthaginian slave on a warship during that time period about 2,200 years ago.

5

And I survived that ordeal. That is the most important point of this experience.

What I have taken from that ancient memory has served me today as Kelvin Chin many times.

I distinctly remember how I "willed" myself to stay alive on that piece of wreckage floating on the Mediterranean. I do not know how long I was on it, but it was long enough for me to feel close to death. Yet I did not give up. I used my mind to keep my body alive. That is what I mean by saying, "I willed myself to stay alive." Eventually I stayed alive long enough for some other vessel, with perhaps some local fishermen, to save me.

But, I have used that knowledge about myself to this day in my 21st century life. The knowledge that my mind and my willpower is so strong that I have the ability — inside myself — to overcome even physical death. Maybe not forever. But in that case 2,200 years ago, long enough to be rescued by the fishermen.

And in this lifetime, I have been laid off five times since I turned 50 years old. Companies or law firms I was working for sometimes got bought by a larger company, so I was let go, laid off and on the street looking for a new job. Other times, the firm ran into difficult financial times, as did many in 2000 and 2008 for example, and I was again on the street. That was extremely stressful first at 50 and finally at 63 — especially when we had a young family we were raising on one income.

The knowledge of my strong mental ability — my will to survive — that I demonstrated in that lifetime 2,200 years ago helped me rekindle the inner strength and confidence I needed each time to get a new job during those multiple layoffs. This was not an easy task in our U.S. culture since employers can easily discriminate based on age without any repercussions, because it is impossible to prove. They just do not call you when they see how many years experience you have. It is as simple as that.

I credit my ability to meet each of those 21st century life challenges on my deep-founded sense of assuredness and confidence based on this ancient knowledge of myself. The conscious awareness that I had looked in the face of death itself and willed myself to survive — albeit 2,200 years ago as a Carthaginian slave — brought a sense of inner calm that I naturally projected in those many job interviews, eventually landing senior positions each time.

Where To Go From Here

My memories did not resurface into my 20th and 21st century conscious awareness in chronological order but here they are in chronological order.

Chapter 2

Sumeria

c. 4000 B.C.

My oldest memory in human history is from ancient Sumeria.

It surfaced when I was in my apartment living in Austin, Texas during a meditation on July 26, 2015. First, without thinking about what I was saying, I spontaneously blurted out: "Jesus was my friend you know, we met in ancient Sumeria." I had no idea those words would come out of my mouth — I actually said them aloud, although I was the only person in my apartment.

My immediate thought after having said that was "Really? I didn't know he had any lifetimes before his life as Jesus." And then I said this aloud: "The nickname you had for him was 'Ashta' or 'Asha.'"

That was it. At least that was all the information I had up to that point so far. I had no idea if that was even a word in Sumerian, but I did not dwell on the thought, I just let it go, and

I let my mind drift on to other things and continued with my meditation.

I then settled into a quiet, settled peacefulness in my meditation. I finished the sitting part of my meditation, then went to my bedroom to lie down for about 15-20 minutes to rest, letting my mind wander to wherever, without focusing or controlling it, similar to the state I am in during the sitting part.

Afterwards I got up, walked right to my laptop and did a Google search for the word "Asha." To my surprise, I found a Sumerian word. It meant "Cosmic Order."

I had never studied Sumerian or any other ancient language, nor had I ever previously looked anything up online about Sumeria or other ancient civilizations of that time period.

This was a complete surprise to me.

The next time I meditated, I had an experience that was also accompanied by a visual — a short video clip — of me standing on my second floor balcony in the early morning talking with an old friend. I was talking with the person I would thousands of years later call "Yeshua," or Jesus.

The stucco balcony was about 50 feet wide and 20-30 feet deep. It was a quiet, serene morning as we both watched the new day's sun rising over the city which was still largely asleep. My family was still asleep, but I was engaged in a quiet but deep philosophical conversation with this old friend. I was a businessman. He was a spiritual teacher.

Chapter 3

Ancient Egypt

c. 3000-1000 B.C.

Museum of Fine Arts

In this 20th century lifetime in the late-1950's when I was 6 or 7 years old, my parents would regularly take my sister and me to visit our grandmother who lived a few blocks across the street from the Museum of Fine Arts in Boston. She would babysit my younger sister, and my dad would go off and do his "guy thing" (probably shopping for accessories for his car, a new chamois to clean his windshield or the latest new car wax), and my mother and I would walk to the museum.

My dad was an early riser, up at 6 AM on workdays or weekends, it didn't matter. So my mom and I would arrive at the museum doorsteps typically 15-20 minutes before it opened on a Saturday morning — standing there rain or shine, snow or humidly hot, waiting right below that life-sized green bronze-oxidized statue in full Native headdress sitting on horseback with his back arched, facing skyward, his arms fully outstretched to each side — thus the name of this 1908 statue, *Appeal to the Great Spirit* — its anonymous, unarmed figure dressed in a mix of Lakota and Diné-style regalia. Even as a 6-year old, I was always struck by the power and majesty of that statue as I waited each visit for the museum doors to open.

So, when they finally unlocked the huge doors, we would walk in with the other early risers — maybe another 6-8 people. Not many. This was decades before museums became popular places to visit.

Even the gift shops back then were tiny. Not the 1,000 square foot shopping extravaganzas that have now become the norm in all big city museums. In 1957, the gift shop...if you could even call it that...was a tiny fraction of that — staffed by one person, and just big enough to sell a few postcards on a swivel stand, some gum and candy, and maybe several pictures of some of the more popular exhibits. Nothing fancy, and certainly not the revenue generators they have become today.

Anyway, we would walk into the museum lobby, and the ritual was always the same. My mom would tell me, "Okay, Kel, now look at Mickey." She was referring to my Mickey Mouse watch. "And when Mickey's little hand (short arm) is on the eleven and his big hand (long arm) is on the twelve, I'll meet you right back here. Okay?"

And she would leave me for two hours to go off and explore the museum by herself — probably the oil paintings because she was a painter back then before my two brothers were born. She even had an exhibit of her own abstract art, her oil paintings in particular, at that very museum in the early 1960's.

11

But, leave me at that age alone in the lobby to explore the museum by myself? No one would ever do that today with a 6-year-old child! If they did, he would probably end up in the city's Child Protective Services. But 1957 was a different time. Leaving me to wander around alone in the Museum of Fine Arts was not seen as odd — not certainly by the museum staff who got used to seeing me there. Maybe it was the times, maybe it was because I looked much older...I had grown very tall since birth and by the time I was 6 years old, I was the height of a 9-year old.

Whatever the reason, I was left alone to explore the museum. Uninterrupted. Wherever I wanted to go.

Here is the strange thing.

Every time I went, I would go to two sections of the museum: the ancient Egyptian artifacts and the medieval armor. I was naturally drawn to them. I cannot explain it any other way. Something about each of those two areas was extremely familiar to me.

All I knew as a young child was that I always felt really comfortable in both of those areas, like I was hanging out with old friends. The hieroglyphs on the papyrus scrolls, carved stone pillars (stelae), mummies, sarcophagi, and the 12th century swords, helmets, chain mail, and even the armor on the huge stuffed warhorses all made me feel as if I was "at home."

Here I was, age 6 or 7 alone in a museum hanging out with 1,000-3,000 year-old ancient Egyptian and medieval artifacts. Feeling as at home with them as I did at my house at 9 Kent Road, Norwood, Massachusetts.

At that age, I didn't think much more about it.

But in retrospect, was that the beginning of my ancient memories starting to be rekindled? Perhaps.

I call those "recognition memories." Sometimes they are the precursors to actual full blown past life memories we may have later.

Memories During Massages

Starting in my late 20's and early 30's, I began remembering several lifetimes in ancient Egypt. I have clear visual memories of being a high priest in at least 3-4 lifetimes. These visions include fairly mundane details of daily life — having makeup put on me, and wearing headdresses and robes. I also recall leading administrative, religious and political activities involved with my role.

In 1980 while being professionally massaged, I began having visions of being massaged in light brown dirt caves, lit by oil lanterns hanging from the walls. It was as if my body had muscle memory that would stimulate my mind's memories. And whenever a massage therapist would start working on my muscles, relieving the tension, it would seemingly release ancient memories from my Egyptian lifetimes.

This repeated many times for several years. Sometimes I had visions and could see scenes, but I knew it was ancient Egypt. Other times there were no specific time or place markings in the scenes, just my knowingness of when and where it was from.

Sex in Caves

In 2009, I began having a memory of having sex with a woman. I am not sure of her social status in ancient Egypt, whether she was a slave or perhaps a princess. Sometimes she appears in my memory to be one and other times she appears as the other, making me wonder if there were two different women, or if they may have been from different lifetimes. Or perhaps she was a princess disguising herself as a slave to be with me. This is a good example of how difficult a seemingly very real experience can be to identify. At any rate, I met many times with that same woman. I was an Egyptian high priest. We would meet secretly in caves lit by oil lamps.

Joseph

When I was in my 40's this lifetime, some time in the 1990's, I started spontaneously saying the following phrase when I was in a relaxed state, "Joseph was a friend of mine." I would just blurt it out, sometimes multiple times. It was not accompanied by any vision or context of any kind. It was just a statement of a deep emotional feeling I had about this person named Joseph — that we were close friends.

I also had the distinct feeling that this friendship was old, maybe even ancient. But at that point, I did not have much more than that to go on.

I happened to mention this on a phone call to my best friend from Dartmouth College, George Hammond. And he said, "Oh really? Do you know who Joseph was?" I said, "No." George said, "I was Joseph."

My first reaction was: Huh? What?

Then, it dawned on me that the ancient feeling that I had, surrounding that simple statement I had been blurting out dozens of times for weeks, may have been connected to what he was talking about.

I began to connect the dots.

Then the memories of being a high priest in ancient Egypt surfaced again, and I realized I had been a very close friend of someone named "Joseph."

I didn't know who Joseph was until George explained the ancient story to me of his being "Yosef" of the many colored robes. "Yosef" is the romanized spelling of the ancient Hebrew name, which we today call Joseph.

That lifetime probably happened within a century or two of 1800 B.C.

Chapter 4

And Now For Something Different

I don't know when the following two lifetimes fit into this historical chronology. So I am putting them way back here among some of my oldest past life memories, because my more "chronologically recent" memories in the past 2,000 years are definitely my clearest ones.

Alien Planet

This was a very clear experience, a vision that I had while I was awake during the restful state after my meditation resting period. I was in a clear, settled "quasi" awake mode, i.e., not asleep or dreaming.

What was most clear was the familiarity and warm emotional bond and recognition of seeing "old friends" again. It felt like a reunion of sorts, after not seeing each other for a very long time. It was accompanied by that comforting inner feeling that, "Oh good, they're all doing well. It's great to see them again…."

I walked out of what I knew to be an inland sea in about calf-deep warm water that felt very soothing and smooth — almost a soft tactile sensation — enveloping my legs and feet. It's not a sensation I ever recall experiencing before in my Earthly lifetimes.

My vehicle was parked behind me stationary in the shallow water about 10-20 yards back (I didn't look back at it, but I knew about how far I had walked from it by this point in the experience) and I was carrying my boots, barefoot. Walking towards my old friends, I saw 3-4 of them about 20 yards away, wading out to greet me from the beach where there were another half dozen standing waving. In the background behind them just off the beach, nestled in the green foliaged, wooded area was a large, low profiled, white geodesic dome.

We were all communicating telepathically with each other, but it felt as if we were all smiling inside. It was joyous to see each other once again.

In the experience, I could not see myself or what was behind me, what the landing craft that was in the water behind me looked like. However, my friends were all tall, with hairless heads, large eyes, two nostril holes but no bone cartilage forming noses like humans have on Earth, and a thin-lipped mouth that could move and open but did not have to be used for speaking. They all wore long white robes, the bottoms of which were getting wet for those who were wading out to greet me.

It felt like a homecoming after a long hiatus elsewhere.

It was about mid-afternoon with clear skies and a comfortable temperature on that world. It wasn't clear to me if I was visiting their planet from another planet, or if I was just visiting them from another region of that same planet. But what was very clear was that this planet was not Earth.

Woman Having Sex

This is also a very clear memory that happened in 1982 while I was in my last year of law school in Boston. I was sleeping alone at the time. My wife was working late at her waitressing job that night, and I had an early morning class.

Around 2:00 AM, I was suddenly awakened and could feel another body penetrating me in the front. I was not sleeping or dreaming, nor was I wide awake. I was in that "twilight state" people sometimes talk of. I did not feel another "presence" in the room. I definitely felt alone by myself. However, I was as if reliving an old memory, but it felt almost "real" because the experience was so vivid.

A large, muscular man was on top of me penetrating me from the front. I was a woman. I could feel him inside me. I had breasts that were noticeable…I could feel them jutting out, rubbing against his chest.

After we finished having sex, the experience dissipated and disappeared. And, back in my 20th century male body, I went right back to sleep. I have no "time markers" from this experience to help me identify a time period for when this lifetime may have occurred because we were naked in the experience with no obvious items, sounds or smells to identify when this may have happened.

Chapter 5

Ancient Babylonia

c. 800 B.C.

Harem

My initial memory of this particular lifetime started dawning in my awareness in the 1990's. I was first aware that I was living in an arid climate as a member of the upper class. I am not sure what my role was in that society. But I explicitly recall having a harem of women.

My memories from this lifetime came piecemeal, and early on I had visions of women's long, hanging earrings, as well as their lightweight gossamer clothing, and especially balloon pants made of very gauzy, see-through material.

Living in a Walled City

On December 11, 2022, during a group meditation with my meditation students, a very clear three-dimensional vision popped up in my mind. All of the shapes and colors were vivid and as real as if I had been awake with my eyes open.

I was walking along behind 12-15 other bearded soldiers along the top of an outer city wall that was about 40-60 feet high and encircled a large city. Looking straight ahead, I estimated the wall extended for about half a mile before it took a turn to the left.

When I looked over the outer side of the wall I could see that the wall seemed even higher than whatever its constructed height was because that part of the wall was built on a section of land that had a drop-off.

We were walking on a roadway about 10-15 feet wide along the top of this city wall. It was constructed to be wide enough for chariots to ride along it and occasionally I could see ruts worn down in the rock surfaces from the chariot wheels. We were wearing loose clothing suitable for the hot, arid climate where we lived. We also wore domed cone-shaped helmets.

I am not sure if this was Babylonia or some city similar to it. But the time period felt very ancient, perhaps around 800 B.C.

Chapter 6

Ancient Greece

c. 500 B.C.

Since I was a child in my 20th century lifetime, I have had an affinity for ancient Greece and Rome.

While my memories of ancient Greece are not as vivid as my Roman ones, I have a strong sense that I did have one or more lifetimes in ancient Greece. It is of course possible, given that my Greek memories are so vague, that my "connection" with Greece could largely be based on my extensive study of Greek culture and philosophy during my life in ancient Rome. So, for those reasons, this lifetime is honestly hard to parse.

My memories are especially filled with discourses and discussions about ancient Greek philosophy. I do have a sense that I was a well-known orator in Greece — that realization occurred when I was standing alone surrounded by Greek artifacts at the Metropolitan Museum of Art in New York City somewhere between 2004 and 2006. Curiously, given my many past life memories in other lifetimes being involved in battles during wars, it is interesting to me that I do not have those types of memories arising from this possible lifetime in ancient Greece.

Chapter 7

Carthaginian Slave

c. 250 B.C.

As I described earlier, one of my first memories to resurface in the late 1970's was as a Carthaginian slave on a warship about 2,200 years ago. This was a vivid memory.

In 1978, I recalled being an African chieftain captured by Carthaginians from my village on the western coast of Africa with my son and many other villagers. At first, I just "knew" we were captured by Carthaginians. I didn't know how I knew that. I just did. I also had a knowingness that we were living along the coast near what is today known as the Ivory Coast.

I had visions of being chased in the area around our village, in the brush and among the trees. They only took the men. Then we were rounded up onto the ships, never to see our homeland again.

We were enslaved and forced to become oarsmen for the Carthaginians on their large warships on the Mediterranean during the Punic Wars. These larger ships had multiple levels of rowing oarsmen all chained down to the floors, as well as to the oars.

I recall we were fed reasonably well, but could die at any moment in battle or even during training exercises. Anyone who was injured beyond easy and immediate repair was killed or simply thrown overboard alive. Our captors figured why waste a morsel of food or a drop of water on someone who is not going to be useful to their fighting needs.

It was a very brutal existence for us slaves. But for those of us who were paying attention, it taught us a lot about human behavior, and life and death — as well as the nature of cruelty and control over others, the impermanence of the human body, the ability of the mind to withstand great physical pain, and where to see glimmers of hope and find peace in the most unlikely moments. In me, it brought about a combined sense of urgency and appreciation for even the smallest, briefest moments of happiness — perhaps at those rare moments when we were allowed on deck for some reason, at night staring up at the starlit skies with the winds peaceful and still. Breathing fresh, pure air. Air untainted by the stench of sweat, vomit, urine, or worse.

I also had further corroboration that this lifetime was during the Punic Wars when I saw in a vision the long planks attached to the enemy ships that came down clamping onto our ships with a large metal hook. I later looked that visual up and learned it was called a *corvus* — or raven — a gangplank with a large metal hook on the end (like the beak of a raven) that when lowered from the ship, then connected it to the enemy ship so the fighting became much more like it was on land. Hand-to-hand close combat.

By using these gangplanks to board the other ship, the soldiers could then tie the ships together and have one huge fighting platform. This neutralized the maneuvering advantage that one ship might have over another while on the open sea.

And which ships had the *corvus* or raven technology?

The Romans. So by inference, that confirmed that I had been on the enemy ships, the Carthaginians.

And when were they invented? Around 260 B.C.

Moreover, they were only used during that first war with the Carthaginians because after gaining the advantage of being able to board their enemy's ships so easily, it leveled the playing field. Consequently, the Romans then had time to develop their as yet undeveloped ship technology. So by the time the next war with the Carthaginians occurred, the Roman shipbuilding technology had outpaced their enemies and they no longer needed to board the ships using the *corvus*.

So — connecting all those dots — I was most likely forced to fight in the First Punic War (264-241 B.C.) as a Carthaginian slave against the Roman navy on the Mediterranean Sea about 2,200 years ago.

Chapter 8

Ancient Hebrew

c. 100 B.C.

In early 1978, I was asked by Maharishi Mahesh Yogi to lead what would end up being my last project for him and his organization. He somehow, as he always seemed to be able to do, found my home phone number (even though it was listed under my apartment mate's name, maybe someone at the local TM center knew whom I lived with) and had one of his personal assistants call me to pass along a message to me from Maharishi. I had just taken a leave of absence from a job in admissions at a college in Boston when, just a few days later, I got that call from him in Switzerland.

Simply put, he wanted me to go to his university located in Fairfield, Iowa to recruit and train a group of Chinese-American meditators to teach TM, then take them to China. I had already taught in Hong Kong several years earlier as its first National Leader of TM, as well as in Korea in the U.S. Army. So, I was already familiar with teaching in Asia and the most logical person to head up this project for him. It sounded like fun, we could do some good work for the world, so I agreed.

When I arrived at Maharishi International University in Fairfield, I was assigned to live with the faculty in their dormitory. I say dormitory, but it really was the first building on "frat row" — a series of a half dozen fraternities built by the previous owners, when it was called Parsons College. So, they were actually pretty comfortable rooms as university living goes.

I knew some of the professors and senior administrators already from various meditation courses I had attended over the previous eight years, so it was a nice reunion. And there were many others with whom I would develop friendships over the subsequent six to seven months.

Every morning and evening we would have a group meditation in one of the large common areas of the faculty "dorm." What we then called our "meditation program" included a few minutes of pranayama (alternate nostril breathing), meditation, then some energy movement mental techniques, followed by a resting period lying down.

During one of the parts of my meditation program — I cannot recall exactly which part — I spontaneously starting blurting out words in a language I did not recognize. Then, at one point while I was meditating with this group, I blurted out the sound "Yahweh" multiple times. I call it a sound, because to me, it was just one of the many "unintelligible sounds" that I was making aloud during those group meditations in the faculty lounge.

This babbling of sounds was involuntary, happening completely on its own accord, as if my vocal chords were uttering them by themselves while I was an observer. Subjectively to me, it felt completely energetic and automatic. Not intellectual at all — with no content understanding or contextual hints.

After one of those sessions, one of the professors came up to me and said, "You know what you're saying in the group meditations?" I said, "No." He told me I was saying, "God" in Hebrew.

It turns out he was Jewish, and he had recognized me from an in-residence 2-month TM teacher meditation retreat we had attended in Switzerland in 1977 (I thought he had looked familiar...). My guess is that others among the 20 or so faculty had also recognized what I was babbling, but perhaps since he felt like he knew me, he was less hesitant to approach me about it.

I had no idea what I had been saying before he clued me in. Where had I learned that word from? I had never studied Hebrew in this 20th century lifetime. Could it have been words resurfacing as memories from the recesses of my mind? Words that I learned in a past life?

My past life memories had started about four months before this "Yahweh" experience. Little did I know that this blurting of Hebrew words would just be near the beginning of — what would end up being — a long list of past life memories.

Chapter 9

Simon Peter

1 B.C.-67 A.D.

M y memories from this lifetime include not only how they arose in my awareness, but also the substance of the teachings that I learned 2,000 years ago from one of my greatest teachers.

Hotel Berghof, Wilderswil, Switzerland

In November 1977, I was attending a two-month in-residence meditation retreat for TM teachers being held at the Hotel Berghof in Wilderswil, Switzerland a few kilometers just outside of Interlaken. There were 75 men in our hotel on this course.

The program consisted of meditating multiple times each day, first several times in our private rooms. Then twice a day all of us would convene in the dining room of the hotel for a large group meditation. The dining room furniture had been previously cleared — then replaced with foam mattresses, each covered with a white sheet, placed wall-to-wall.

During those group meditations, we practiced what was called the TM-Siddhi program which involved mental repetition of certain yoga sutras of Patanjali, a Vedic seer who wrote them about two thousand years ago in 200 B.C. Essentially, we were practicing a form of energy movement — the technique would cause energy rushes making our bodies move in various ways.

The most common movement would be hopping. So you would have seen a bunch of guys sitting cross-legged "frog-hopping" across the foam mattresses as the energy rushes would shoot up along their spines through their bodies. Some called it "flying" but it was actually hopping, if even that.

Furthermore, not everyone even hopped. Some people just sat still and experienced whatever they experienced, perhaps energy flow or expansion of one's conscious awareness — who knows what they were experiencing internally — but externally they just sat still. And others would mostly sit still, but move occasionally when an energy burst occurred. It was quite an amusing scene with lots of hopping, twitching, squirming with an occasional yelp or screech peppered in there for good measure.

I did some of all three possibilities. But mostly I moved a lot and sometimes hopped. I had a lot of energy flowing and bursting — as if through barriers — throughout my body and mind.

Everyone was different.

For me, the really big energy bursts started one night in my bedroom when I was woken up at 3:30 AM by a jolt of energy that shot through my entire body. I proceeded to repeatedly do "half sit ups" every few seconds for about 2 to 3 hours all night.

They were involuntary movements of my body caused by the energy bursting through it. You might think that after doing so many sit ups my stomach muscles would be exhausted and tighten up, but they did not — they just felt normal when I got up that morning.

That is how it started for me. Like I said, everyone's experience was different.

However, during one of the group meditations while all this activity was going on all around me, I had an unusual experience where I spontaneously flipped over onto my back.

Picture this — I start with my eyes closed, beginning to do the internal mental technique, sitting normally with my legs crossed, then suddenly without any warning, energy shoots through me, my legs involuntarily become uncrossed and go straight back over my head, pushing my back down flat onto the mattress, while at the same time, both my arms spontaneously fly out to the sides. I am flipped over, lying back on my shoulders in a partial upside down position. That's what happened to me on the outside. As I said, this all happened in a split second, completely automatically without any warning.

Inside, I am experiencing tremendous physical pain and deep emotional anguish. At first I do not have any recognition or realization what this is from. All I know is that the internal experience is very intense.

At times, I scream out loud involuntarily. I just can't help it. I am yelling and moaning in pain.

So, I am observing the experience as it occurs. It is very strong as I mentioned, but I am not overwhelmed by the experience. My awareness of my individual consciousness — the "experiencer" — as separate and distinct from my "experiences" is well established by then.

By November 1977, I had been meditating consistently every day at least twice a day for seven years. In addition, I had already been on many weekend, week-long, month-long retreats, as well as a six-month long one, where we meditated all day, every day. Consequently, I had developed a fairly unshakeable connection within myself which allowed me to experience intense experiences without becoming overwhelmed by them.

After several days of this odd experience happening for entire hour-long group meditations, I had the realization that I was being crucified upside down. Or, maybe more accurately, I was experiencing the memory of having been crucified in an inverted position. I somehow knew that is what the physical and emotional pain was associated with.

This continued happening every time I meditated in the group. Day after day. My body continued to flip over into that inverted position. All on its own.

Okay, before I continue, here are a few additional contextual points so that the experience that followed will be easier to understand.

Meeting My Brother Again

Another part of our regular daily program was to go for "walk and talks" with a buddy we selected at the beginning of the two-month meditation retreat. The purpose of the buddy system was to keep an eye on each other to make sure your buddy was making it to meals, group meditations and to have someone to talk with on your twice daily walks after lunch and dinner. Since we were meditating most of each day, interspersed with sets of yoga and pranayama breathing techniques, getting out twice a day for an hour each time to get a little more physical exercise walking in the hills and trails around our hotel was seen as a necessary and healthful component to our daily regimen.

My buddy on this course was George Hammond. He and I had met at Dartmouth College in 1971 when he was a freshman and I was a junior. We happened to live in the same dorm, Wheeler Hall. And maybe not so coincidentally, I introduced his Transcendental Meditation (TM) meditation teacher at his introductory lecture, in my role as the founding president of SIMS-Dartmouth (Students International Meditation Society).

A few weeks after that lecture, on a Saturday afternoon when most of the students were at the Dartmouth football game across campus, I happened to glance at my dorm window in 212 Wheeler and saw a curious thing happening. I saw a frisbee going up and down, up and down. From its trajectory I could tell it was someone playing frisbee by himself. Sure enough, when I walked closer to the window and looked down at the lawn, there was this guy throwing a frisbee to himself.

I called down to him, not recognizing him, and said jokingly, "Hey, do you want to play frisbee *with someone*?" So, that is how we first met, although George said he recognized me from having introduced the speaker at his meditation lecture a couple weeks earlier.

A year later while he was a Dartmouth sophomore, George took a semester off to complete his TM teacher training with Maharishi Mahesh Yogi. I subsequently graduated early from college, then flew to Europe to complete my training with Maharishi in Spain. George took over as the second president of SIMS-Dartmouth. Together, we were jointly responsible for 600 new TM meditators at Dartmouth over a two-year period.

After I graduated from Yale Graduate School in 1974, George and I reunited in Switzerland at a Vedic Studies course with Maharishi. Then afterwards we again worked and lived together in Hong Kong, where we, along with the native speakers we trained there, taught meditation to several thousand people.

Suffice it to say, that George and I have developed a very close friendship this lifetime. And by the time we were in the Hotel Berghof on that course in 1977, we knew each other very well.

But, little did I know at that point, how well George knew me.

Remembering Who I Was...

So back to the crucifixion experience…

After a couple of weeks of reliving being crucified like this during every meditation, I went with George on one of our daily afternoon "walk and talks," along the bucolic path up the hillside behind the hotel. As we walked past several cows grazing lazily in the nearby fields, I said, "George, I had this really intense dream about 6-8 months ago…."

I was just about to tell him the details of it when he abruptly interrupted me and described my dream to me in great detail. He told me exactly the way I looked in it, what I was wearing, where I was, and how I was feeling in it.

I was shocked. Dumbfounded. Speechless.

George had just recounted to me everything I had experienced in the dream months earlier back in my apartment in Boston. After he finished the dream that I had only begun to tell him, he said,

"You don't know who you are?"

I said, "No, what are you talking about?"

George said, "Well, you know how you've been saying that you're experiencing being crucified every time in our group meditations for the last two weeks?" I said, "Yeah." He said,

"And you know how you've been experiencing being crucified *upside down*? You don't know who was crucified *upside down*?"

I said, "No." He said, "You're Peter."

He told me Peter (Simon Peter) had requested to be crucified upside down because he did not consider himself worthy of being crucified in the same way Jesus had been.

I was raised Christian. More specifically, we went to the First Congregational Church in Norwood because my mom liked Reverend Keedy ("...he seems like a very nice man," she said) when he came and knocked on the "new neighbors" door, soon after we moved in. Plus he had a young son, Allen, with whom my mom figured I, then age 5, could start having "play dates." So it was a win-win from my mom's perspective.

But I didn't pay attention in Sunday school. My sister and I went to Sunday school each week because our parents told us we had to. As I got older, I was more interested in the cute girls in my Sunday school class than I was the Bible readings. Sure, I took my turn in class reading the Bible passages aloud. But the substance of the stories didn't resonate with me. They just seemed like stories some people had made up and collected into something they called the "Bible." The person named Jesus we read about seemed like a good guy, but to me as a kid growing up in that setting, he was a man. Not a "god."

George, on the other hand, had grown up in Kenosha, Wisconsin. He was the fourth child in a Catholic family of twelve children who were raised by devout Catholic parents. His father even became a deacon in their local church, and his mother had originally planned on becoming a nun before she changed her mind and got married. He had been an altar boy from age 8 to 14 and had attended Catholic schools through his high school graduation before I met him at Dartmouth College.

So unlike me, George was steeped in Biblical stories and personal experience with the church and its Christian traditions.

He said to me, "You know how you've been saying for the past two weeks you feel like you're being crucified upside down? You're Peter. Peter was crucified upside down."

When he said that, something in me clicked. I got a rush of energy that shot through my body from my feet out through the top of my head. I was buzzing energetically, standing on that dirt path among the grazing cows.

We continued to chat about this. How the dream I had had six to eight months earlier of being so distraught lying in the ditch along the side of the dirt road was connected to that lifetime.

George revealed to me that his past life memories had begun opening up a couple years earlier when we were teaching meditation together living in Hong Kong. And that he remembered he was my brother Andrew in that lifetime 2,000 years ago, but did not want to tell me until I started having my own memories independently.

It all started to make sense.

Why I had felt so upset, crying, lying in that ditch and about whom?

Every time I meditated for about six months afterwards, for at least part of the meditations I would continue to flip over on my back and feel like I was being crucified. The pain gradually subsided over time — both emotionally and physically. However, the energetic reaction to the memory persisted and the body contortions in my meditations continued.

Over those months, there seemed to be almost an inverse proportional relationship between my pain and my memories.

While the emotional and physical pain gradually subsided, my memories of that lifetime increased and became clearer. Could it have been that my past experiences of emotional and physical pain had been blocking my memories?

I had a vision of walking with my wife and some friends 2,000 years ago down a dusty road between two walls, off-white stucco type walls, approximately 6 to 8 feet high on each side of the road. I knew the time period both intuitively and from the robes and other types of clothing we wore.

I began to have clear memories of speaking to small and large groups of people, both on the streets of Judea, on the hillsides, in homes and in the catacombs. I observed that I could speak and explain the teachings in a way that people could understand. I saw that I was able to "translate" complex ideas into plain language that was intelligible to the layperson on the street, regardless of their education, social status, age, gender or religion.

Then, I began to remember my times walking and talking with Jesus.

At first the memories came as feelings, which they still do from time to time. Feelings of how I felt with him in certain situations. Not clear recollections of conversations, or of specific words exchanged, but more how I felt emotionally at the time in those situations with him.

I was often — and it still happens sometimes — brought to tears recalling how brutally he was murdered. I was haunted for many years by that horrific event, how we heard about it from others who witnessed it, and how I may have contributed to it. But I have since resolved my inner conflict about my role, with his help through a number of visitations from him, over the past 10 years.

John the Baptist Meets Jesus

One of my memories from that lifetime is seeing a long line of people waiting to be baptized by John (the Baptist). I was a student of John's having been introduced to him by my brother Andrew.

In this vision that happened during or after a meditation, I could see myself sitting on a hillside high up on a large rocky area. I was perched on a huge 12-15 foot rock or pile of similarly large rocks overlooking a canyon area with a river running through it. John was standing in the river about waist deep approximately 150-200 feet away from me. The line of people to be baptized wound up along a path through the canyon.

I remember that John excitedly told us afterwards that he had met Jesus. That as soon as Jesus, who had also been standing in that long line, and he locked eyes, they knew who each other was and the role they each were to play in the "project."

Even though they were distant cousins — John the Baptist's mother Elizabeth and Jesus's mother Mary were cousins — they had not spent time with each other growing up. And now they were both young men in their early 30's, John being a couple years older than Jesus. Both were spiritual teachers here to express and share their teachings with us.

So shortly after that, John told Andrew and me, as well as a number of others, that we should go with Jesus and study with him. We did.

I don't recall seeing John alive again after that. Tragically, he was beheaded by Herod.

I am guessing that John's personality trait of "righteous indignation," which was often on display especially when people did not follow his teachings and advice properly, was a factor in his premature death. That said, angering Herod or his wife was also not difficult to do. And that ultimately was the cause of my old friend and teacher John the Baptist's demise. Herod, his wife and their daughter Salome bear that responsibility in the end.

Seeking the Kingdom of Heaven Within

When we were with Jesus, he taught us how to meditate. He called it, "Seeking the kingdom of heaven within." It was an internal process we all did with him with our eyes closed. It was not the same as praying which had content to the process, where we would think about certain things or ask for guidance.

His process of seeking within was a content-less process, which today I would view as meditative. We would each allow our minds to experience itself, the vastness of itself, which is why he called it the "kingdom of heaven." That expression was his way of describing that inner experience. It was not a description of some external location. He was not describing "heaven" as a place to go to after one died. He was talking about a "place" within each of us to contact and establish connection with *while we were alive*.

Jesus already knew how to "meditate" in this way. He didn't have to travel anywhere to learn it from someone else. It seemed to me that he either was born with knowing how, or that he figured it out along the way before we met him.

Walking With Jesus

I have since had many memories of walking with Jesus along dusty roads, meeting with people, discussing and giving lectures to large groups of people.

I also have memories of Jesus visiting us at my mother-in-law's house, holding our infant child who is now my current daughter, Sam. It was a one- or two-room house which was common in the 1st century in that region. My brother Andrew lived with us — meaning he had a cot to sleep on. Most homes were very basic in those days — a place to sleep, cook, eat and be sheltered from the elements.

My most powerful memory of him was Jesus's ability to connect deeply with every person he met. For him it was innate. Automatic. Natural. I observed that and have aspired to develop that similar ability over the past 2,000 years in my own relationships — both with loved ones and with strangers.

He could do that seamlessly. It was a miracle to watch, to observe.

He could "see" who they were, their soul, their deepest thoughts and desires. And he would quickly assess and act accordingly.

To me, that is the greatest gift I learned from him. How to begin to do that.

Because that is "love."

Jesus's View on Love

He said, "Love is accepting the other person for who they are, not who you wish they were."

As I said, he did that automatically, without thinking. Just in his being.

That is why you hear so many people say, "Jesus is love." It is not meant to be literal. It is an expression of how he interacted with the external world.

By accepting it.

Now, was he perfect at it? No. Because we saw him get frustrated and angry over time when the masses were not paying attention to his teachings about "going within to seek the kingdom of heaven," for example. It also bothered him deeply when he saw people still judging others by their external material possessions, continuing to ignore his messages about going within to find lasting happiness, instead using their possessing (or giving up) of their external stuff as some measurement of virtue.

That frustration led to his doing miracles, which my brother Andrew convinced me was a mistake. Because it put more emphasis on Jesus's ability to heal than on his original messages of teaching people how to heal themselves by "seeking the kingdom of heaven within."

But again, was Jesus a powerful being? Absolutely yes. Was he a loving being? Absolutely yes.

And were his teachings derailed and disrupted by his premature death? Absolutely yes.

Jesus's teachings were derailed by Paul.

Paul's Derailment of the Teaching

Who was Paul, really?

I knew Paul. I liked him. He had a charismatic personality.

Paul never met Jesus. Paul joined us in our teaching efforts about three and a half years after Jesus died.

Before that, Paul had been a tax collector and persecutor of those Jews who were followers of Jesus and his teachings. Somewhere walking on the road to Damascus, Paul said he had a vision of Jesus who asked him why he was persecuting his people.

Some time after that, Paul came to us and asked us about Jesus's teachings. Since he had never been in his presence while Jesus was alive in physical form, and had therefore never heard any of his teachings first-hand, he asked us, who had been with Jesus, to share those teachings with him. So when we realized that Paul was sincerely interested, we gladly shared them with him.

While Paul was not one of the original apostles who traveled, taught, and ate and laughed with Jesus, he did begin teaching Jesus's messages that we taught him.

I say "begin teaching," because about fifteen years later, in approximately 48-50 A.D., it somehow got back to us that Paul had stopped teaching Jesus's teachings. And instead, he had evidently concocted his own teaching that Jesus had died on the cross for everyone else's sins, and that all you had to do was believe that, in order for you to get a "free pass" to go to the head of the line to "get admitted into heaven."

What?!

To put it mildly, we were shocked and aghast. And angry that Jesus's teachings — which we grew to realize were so important for the progress of humanity — were being usurped by someone who never even knew Jesus. Many of us began to question Paul's intentions, wondering if he was in fact a willing usurper, never intending to be a teacher of Jesus.

So, Jesus's brother James, who was head of the Jerusalem church, convened a meeting. And word was sent out by messengers to all of us apostles to come back to Jerusalem to discuss our progress in our respective regions. Paul also received that message.

Because we were spread out as many as hundreds of miles apart, it took us several weeks to all get back. Remember that we mostly walked everywhere, with an occasional ride on a cart or on a burro, or by boat if near the river or sea. So traveling long distances was slow and arduous.

Eventually, we all returned to Jerusalem for this meeting. The main focus was to share our progress. However, I was extremely irate with Paul for his radical change of the teachings and telling people this whole horrible fantasy about Jesus's murder. After all, these were people who trusted Paul and who would otherwise have no other way of knowing whether Paul was telling the truth or not.

I called Paul out at the meeting. As I said, I had previously liked Paul. He was a very charismatic character. He could be very persuasive. And he was a bright guy.

But he had been lying to the people about Jesus's teachings. So, I got into a shouting match with Paul at the meeting. We all felt betrayed by Paul.

Somehow Paul had created a story from that vision he had while traveling to Damascus — that Jesus was "the Christ" who died on the cross to save everyone who believed in that story.

Paul made that story up.

He used the term "Christ" which is Greek, because Paul was a Greek-speaking Jew. It means "Messiah" in Greek.

Jesus never called himself Christ. Nor would he ever see himself that way. Jesus was a humble man. Powerful yes, but centered and grounded in that power within himself. Not arrogant. And he never sought or saw himself as a king figure, never mind a Messiah. He saw himself as a teacher, which is the way he still sees himself.

However, after James convened that meeting and we had that heated discussion in Jerusalem, Paul agreed to stop spreading his own teachings in the name of Jesus, and he agreed to go back to teaching Jesus's actual messages. So we all left that meeting feeling better, and went back out into our respective areas and continued teaching what Jesus had taught us. Paul seemed sincere and genuine in his apology and pledge to us that he would discontinue his false teachings immediately.

Unfortunately, Paul lied to us, and we later heard that, notwithstanding his promise to all of us when we met in

Jerusalem, he had gone out and continued to preach that fantasy that he had created. I was furious — he betrayed my friendship with him. I took his deceit as a personal affront to our friendship, our relationship.

Paul's insecurities created that "story" about Jesus. Nothing more.

Paul was an insecure person, wanting desperately to be recognized and known, and was I think jealous of those who had actually been with Jesus. It is too bad, because as I have said, I liked Paul, and I think he could have been a great asset to helping us spread Jesus's teachings.

Remember, not all of the dozens of apostles teaching throughout the region had met or been with Jesus in person. Yet I made sure we treated everyone equally. There was no pecking order, no hierarchy to worry about. Teaching was our focus, not organizational politics.

We were not starting a new religion. We were teaching principles that would help all of humanity. That is what inspired us.

However, Paul's insecurity and narcissism, I think, became his ruling inner compass. Consequently, he chose a different path.

I never heard from or saw him again.

Many Apostles

There were many "apostles" who spread out to the surrounding areas, far and wide, to teach Jesus's teachings. There were more than the "Twelve Apostles."

My recollection is that there may have been as many as several dozen of us teaching in villages and homes, initially in Judea and eventually throughout what we now know as the Middle East, northern Africa, and eastern Europe. This includes

Miriam of Magdala (known by most as "Mary Magdalene") and other women who also acted as apostles, although in a more low key way given the culture of that time.

Seeing Jesus After His Crucifixion

My memories with Jesus not only include being with him when he was alive, but also with him after he physically biologically died.

After Jesus died on the cross, he visited with many of us.

When I say "many," I am not just referring to those of us who were his teachers. In fact, he came and spoke to about 500 to 1,000 of us on a hillside after he died, so that many people of all walks of life could see him in his "energy body." When I say he had an energy body, it was a body of shimmering light that took the shape and features of his former biological body so we could recognize his face and his form, however it was made of energy, not flesh. He also visited some of us in small groups and even alone shortly after his crucifixion, so we could chat with him. I estimate that he visited about 10-12 times in those few weeks right after his death.

Why did he do that?

To demonstrate to us that the mind or soul continues after we each biologically die. To help us overcome the fear of death.

To help us live life here free from fear.

Because that in fact was the objective of the John the Baptist-Jesus Project that we planned together on the Other Side before we each incarnated that lifetime 2,000 years ago.

The Shock of His Death

I remember how shocked we all were after Jesus was murdered. Even though he visited us which made us feel better knowing that he was still "alive," he was not physically with us anymore. He was still "dead" and not with us every day. Simply put, it was not as easy to talk and be with him. Each of us had our own relationship with him, so each of us grieved in our unique, personal ways.

There were many thousands who were touched by his presence when he was here teaching, and when I say we each grieved in our own personal ways, I am referring to those thousands, not just the twelve apostles. I recall how traumatized many of them were when they saw how he was treated and then murdered. People on the street I did not even know were shocked. I remember their faces, their eyes, their energy. It was not only a traumatic event for Jesus, but also traumatic for all who were there and continued living after he was gone. We were all deeply affected, every one of the thousands he touched.

I also know who some of the several dozen apostles are today in the 21st century. Many of them are still so traumatized by the horrific experience of Jesus's crucifixion, even though it was 2,000 years ago, that they still are unable or unwilling to discuss it, or have anything to do with furthering his teaching. I also know some who are still carrying the burden of his death in today's lifetime in how it is affecting their relationships with others. But, for the most part what many learned from him is often being expressed by them in helping others in their various communities, albeit in a quiet, more private way. Consequently, in whatever way I can, I continue to help people who were with him understand and process the shock of what they witnessed 2,000 years ago.

Teaching in Rome

After Jesus was murdered, most of the teachers scattered to the four winds to spread his teachings to as many people as they could. Some, however, were so immediately traumatized by his crucifixion that they found it emotionally difficult to continue teaching.

As I have said, there were many of us teaching, not just the twelve apostles. Some of us went to different countries to continue our mission. My brother Andrew went to Greece.

I remember going to Rome with my daughter where we both taught. I recall teaching in the catacombs. And, I viscerally remember — having mentally relived the horrible experience again this lifetime — being crucified in Rome, which was ordered by the emperor Nero. I was in my late 60's when I died there.

Jesus and Divinity

Jesus was first and foremost our teacher. The incisiveness of his mind has been lost in the storybooks. His intellect was impressive.

Yes, he was a loving man. However, he expressed that love not only through his feelings towards you, but also in his excitement to teach you new ideas and ways of thinking, and how to "turn within" and connect with one's self.

He also saw himself as neither a guru, nor a god. He demanded nothing from any of us. He merely made himself available "for those who had ears to hear." And we definitely wanted to hear what he had to say. However, he never encouraged blindly following him. That is not to say that some who were his students didn't view him that way — as a guru or a god walking on Earth. But that was *their* perception of him, not *his* perception of himself. And most certainly, not his desire to be perceived that way by us.

He wanted us to see him as a teacher. Someone who could share ideas and perspectives with us. Someone who was more or less our equal, though perhaps wiser in certain areas and willing to share that wisdom with us. That's how he expressed himself to us. How others viewed him then, and subsequently, was not within his control.

I know that aspect of how he viewed himself and how he treated us when we were with him has left a deep and lasting impression in me all these years. Because, while I have not been completely immune to following religious or spiritual authoritarians, I have tried to maintain a healthy distance from those who have tended to be "blind followers" of those spiritual leaders, as well as regularly questioning those leaders myself. I owe my having developed that "ability to discern" to my teacher Jesus who always demanded, at least implicitly and sometimes explicitly, that we think for ourselves.

Jesus and Friendship

One of my deepest memories is being his friend and how good a friend he was to me, and those he was closest to. The deepest impression and memory I have of him was how deeply he could connect with you, no matter who you were.

Of all the things he taught me, that was the most important. It did not matter to him what your station in life was — rich or poor, young or old, healthy or infirm, male or female, Jew or non-Jew. He connected with you — your mind, heart, soul — all of the above. In an instant.

That ability to connect is why I think most people remember him as an embodiment of "love." Because love is about accepting and connecting. To me, that was his very nature, it was how he was wired, it was innate for him. And still is.

Those lessons and memories began to cascade into my conscious awareness after November 1977.

Jesus Visitation — Monarch Apartments

My most vivid visitation from Jesus happened in Spring 2014 before Easter while I was meditating in my living room at the Monarch, an apartment building in downtown Austin, Texas. While I was sitting with my eyes closed, I saw him in his life-size form in front of me. It was an odd experience in that my eyes were physically closed, however I could see him and some of my surroundings as if my eyelids were open.

His face was full-size, three-dimensional and positioned about a foot away from mine, the same distance a close friend would be if he or she was talking with you about something personal. And he was kneeling in front of me, talking with me. I could see his entire form from head to toe. He looked and sounded as real as I remembered him from 2,000 years ago in Jerusalem, except he was in my living room in present day 2014 Austin.

While this occurred during my meditation soon after I closed my eyes, I obviously immediately turned my attention to the conversation he began with me. To be clear, this happened spontaneously without any warning. It is true that I had been organizing the 30th November Talk at his and others' request for a few months before this visit. But I had no forewarning that he was going to visit me alone in this way.

He spoke with me about what I had done 2,000 years ago after we parted ways in the Garden of Gethsemane, the small olive grove where he was arrested the night before he was killed. Jesus said there was no need for him to forgive me for having denied knowing him three times that night as he had predicted, because he said his love for me was all that mattered, and that he never stopped loving me. Then he reminded me what he had taught us when we studied with him: that "love is accepting the other person for who they are, not who you wish they were." And he reminded me that he always loved me in that way — accepting me with all my flaws as well as my strengths.

When he spoke with me about this, I was speechless. All I could do was sob. I cried throughout this conversation with him in my apartment. I felt his love, his complete acceptance of me, and what I had done…and that it didn't matter to him.

That experience of having denied him that night had haunted me for 2,000 years not far below the surface, and it finally started to lift.

The conversation took place entirely telepathically. I was not speaking out loud to him, but I could "hear" his words as thoughts in my mind as clearly as if someone were physically in a body in my room using their vocal chords talking to me.

Jesus spoke with me about our deep friendship. And how that friendship could never be shaken by any transgression that either of us might do to the other.

At that point in the experience, I was crying so much that I got up from my chair, walked to my bedroom and laid down and continued to cry…and to digest the words he had spoken to me.

After some time, maybe around 20 minutes, I got up, made some dinner, ate, then went downstairs to my apartment swimming pool outside. As was usual at the Monarch, I was often the only one using the pool, especially at night, so I swam some laps, then relaxed floating on my back.

At that point, Jesus came back and finished his conversation with me. He had left earlier when we were upstairs because he knew I was so upset and crying so much that I would not have been able to take in the rest of the conversation he wanted to have with me.

So while I was alone floating on my back in the pool, he talked with me about "friendship." And how precious friendship is. And how the world is lacking in friendship — true friendship in the way he described to me. Friendship based on love. Love as acceptance in the way he had already defined and reminded me of how he taught us to think of it 2,000 years ago.

He asked me to teach that perspective on love and friendship to others.

I'm sure he had by then — from the Other Side — heard me blurt out the phrase, "Jesus was my friend, ya know" thousands of times since my children were infants (Sam reminded me recently that it is one of her oldest memories this lifetime). It is a phrase I have spontaneously said out loud in my quiet moments, especially as I was getting ready to meditate or lying down to go to sleep, since the late 1980's to early 1990's. I don't know why it comes out when it does, but it is undoubtedly an expression of my subconscious memory of that deep friendship we had and still have.

Jesus Visitation — Round Rock, Texas

In May 2017, while I was taking a shower at my ex-girl-friend's mother's house in Round Rock, Jesus came to me another time. He again spoke to me about the concept of love. But this time he elaborated on it, saying that love can take on many different forms and expressions. That while it has a common underpinning as he defined it to us 2,000 years ago and which he reminded me of in my apartment three years earlier, he said, "Love has many nuances to it that need to be explained and illustrated to people."

He asked me to give talks and lead discussions about that. Because he said while he had intended to share his ideas on the subject as one of the several projects on his plate 2,000 years ago, he was only here for those three to four years before his unanticipated death, so he did not have time to get to it.

He also said to me, "Plus, you have a lot more experience than I ever had with relationships, so you can speak sharing examples with people that they will understand."

Jesus Visitation — Hawthorne, California

In 2020, while I was writing several essays on "Love," "Forgiveness" and a number of other topics for my second book, Jesus came to me again to remind me of his definition of love. He also reminded me of how he taught us to draw boundaries. He pointed out in his maxim that is often cited from the gospel according to Matthew in the Bible, and that my good friend George Hammond (who was my brother Andrew 2,000 years ago) also cites in his *Gospel According to Andrew*: "Behold, I send you forth as sheep in the midst of wolves: be ye therefore wise as serpents, and harmless as doves." (Matthew 10:16)

Jesus warned that the part about being "wise as serpents" is often forgotten, especially by people who are loving and empathetic. And that those very loving people are often hurt by cruel people who take advantage of those who forget to heed Jesus's first piece of advice in the sentence. It is as if they let their guard down, and have no boundaries when they only follow the last part of his advice to be "harmless as doves." He reminds and admonishes those of us who forget the "wise as..." instruction that we are only following half of his teaching, and thereby exposing ourselves to unnecessary suffering.

A Recognition Memory in France

In retrospect, I have wondered if another recognition memory — a precursor to my Simon Peter recollections — may have occurred when I was studying in France at the Université de Strasbourg in 1971. That would have been six years before my Simon Peter memories started to resurface.

I was a French major in college. Having studied the language starting in the 5th grade, by the time I graduated from high school, with the help of some excellent French teachers (Mrs. Johngren and Mrs. Staton) I was well prepared for my university classes and fairly fluent in French.

So, as a freshman at Dartmouth College, having taken the College's own in-house placement test when we arrived on campus, I found myself in advanced French literature classes, having tested out of the first several years of language training. (As a side note, I later heard from one of my classmates that we shared a small French literature class when we were freshmen with an upperclass(wo)man who was visiting Dartmouth in 1970 from Vassar College, a blonde girl named Meryl Streep.)

In the Spring of my sophomore year while we were studying in France, one of our classes was on French Art and Architecture. For that class, we were required to write a term paper. Most of the guys (Dartmouth was all male at that time, except for the occasional visiting female student from another college) picked one of the many historic and elaborate cathedrals or castles as their subject, researching popular topics like *les voûtes d'arêtes* — the unique arches often appearing in Gothic architecture — or the "flying buttresses" at the famed Notre-Dame de Paris.

However, what did I choose to write about? Something obvious like those many amazing edifices still existent throughout France — rich in history, design and construction?

Or perhaps some paintings by some of the most renowned artists in Western history — Monet, Degas, Matisse, Renoir or Gauguin?

Of course not.

One day our group of twenty Dartmouth students went on a field trip to a museum in Colmar, a small French town with cobblestone streets lined with medieval and early Renaissance buildings about one hour (70 km) almost directly south of Strasbourg, just across from the German border. The curator took us on a private tour of his museum, *La Musée Unterlinden*, which was originally located in a 13th century convent. Among other artifacts, the museum is known for certain religious pieces, especially the Altarpiece of Isenheim created for a monastery nearby, as well as many other works of art from 1300-1500 depicting various figures from Christianity, most notably of course Jesus, Mother Mary, and various apostles.

So, during the tour, I struck up a conversation in French with the curator. I expressed my interest in writing my term paper on some of the artwork in his museum. And I asked him if he would help me with understanding the rich history behind a selection of certain pieces — especially information that would not be easily found in research books (remember, this was 1971, long before the age of computers, so research meant looking up information in card catalogs at libraries and reading through hundreds of pages of multiple books to find the "needle in the haystack" information gems you were looking for).

He agreed. In fact, he expressed excitement at the prospect of helping me, as nobody had ever asked him for his help in this particular way before.

We made an appointment for me to take a train back and spend the day "picking his brain." I was excited at the prospect of drawing upon his expertise, in a matter of hours what had taken years for him to study and learn, about all the ancient pieces of art under his purview at his museum.

A few days later as we walked through the museum, he and I began to focus on certain religious art pieces, especially those around Jesus and his crucifixion. This particular museum had many pieces devoted to and commemorating that horrible event in Jesus's life.

However, for some — at that time — unknown reason, I was fascinated by learning as much as I could about crucifixions from this museum curator, who I quickly learned had a particularly extensive wealth of knowledge about crucifixions. In fact, at one point he paused, and asked me, "Do you know what happens when you are crucified?"

He asked me if there was a playground near where I lived. I said, my French family has kids so there was a swing set in our backyard. In French he said, "Perfect. Now when you go back home this afternoon, stretch your arms out to each side, hold onto the bars, and try to hang there suspended with your feet off of the ground. See how long you can do that. You won't be able to do it for very long, because you will begin to suffocate…your lungs will start to feel so much pressure from your body being in that position, that you will increasingly find it more and more difficult to breathe. It is a horrible way to die. And to make it even more horrible, they would sometimes put an angled piece of wood for the subject to stand on, but since it was angled they would gradually keep slipping on it…they could not put all their body weight on it to rest…it was just a tease to keep them alive longer so their torture would be more intense and more drawn out. So cruel. And that's if they *tied* you to the wooden cross beam, not nail your hands and feet like they did to poor Jesus."

I learned a lot in that short afternoon visit with this man, the curator of that museum. And sure enough, as soon as I got back home to my family's house in the suburbs of Strasbourg, I went right to the backyard and tried to hang suspended in that position, and after just a few minutes found it difficult to breathe.

Crucifixions existed in Europe and the Middle East throughout the Roman Empire, for 500 years until they were banned by the Roman Emperor Constantine. Such cruelty at the expense of what? It has stuck with me ever since as something I have been committed to lessening in the world — that is, teaching the need to "Transcend Cruelty."

What are the odds? The curator of the museum just happened to not only have specific expertise about the wide array of art works under his supervision, which would make sense of course, but also an unusual body of knowledge about the religious pieces and those depicting crucifixions in particular.

How serendipitous for me to stumble upon him to help me fulfill my curiosity about the subject. And how odd that the subject might eventually surface in my life as a resurfacing of an ancient memory of my own, a mere six years later in 1977 in Wilderswil, Switzerland.

So let's continue with more of those other past lives that I started resurfacing memories from…. This next lifetime began after I was on the Other Side for about fifty years.

Chapter 10

Marcus Aurelius

121-180 A.D.

The Mosaic

I was raised in Norwood, Massachusetts, a suburb of Boston which then had a population of around 20,000 people. We moved there from our first home in Natick when I was 4 years old. It turns out many other new families were also moving to that well-established New England town, for its ambience as a suburb just on the edge of the wooded rural farmlands, focused on good childhood education, along with a train station that had a direct line to Boston only 30 minutes away.

So, there was a lot of new housing development going on due to the influx of those new families who also found the proximity to Route 128 an attractive commuting feature. And new housing development and new families meant new schools.

Some of us were doubled up for a couple years at existing schools until the new schools could be finished. Finally, my class moved into the brand new Cleveland Elementary School, which was an easy, relaxing, safe walk through our residential neighborhood that took only 10-15 minutes...even with our short, little 7-year old legs.

My class entered the new elementary school in 2nd grade. About a month into the school year, a half dozen of us were allowed to skip certain sections of class that we had already mastered.

To keep us engaged creatively and intellectually, our school principal came up with the idea of having us work on our own independent project that would be supervised by the town art teacher. He was the sole art teacher for the town's half dozen elementary schools, who traveled from school to school every day teaching art classes. Little did he know at the time, but he was one of the trailblazers of what would become commonplace 70 years later — working remotely!

So, the six of us 2nd graders convened in the large brand new common room outside of our classroom. Our art teacher told us we were going to make something called a "mosaic." He explained to us that a mosaic is a collection of small tiles attached together to make a design. He then left us to come up with an idea for our mosaic.

I suggested to our small group that we recreate an underwater scene. We first drew the design on a large piece of paper the size of the eventual mosaic itself, each contributing different parts of the overall scene — fish, plants, sea floor. I specifically recall making the large yellow fish, then I taught others how to create the smaller ones.

When I was young, I regularly visited my mom's parents at their 5-story walkup (104 Tyler Street adjacent to Boston's

Chinatown), where my grandfather had his noodle factory in the basement. Upstairs was where the family of ten lived, where my mom and her seven siblings grew up. My Uncle Arnold who was 15 when I was born had as many as thirty very large 60-gallon fish tanks full of different kinds of fresh water fish and plants (he and my grandfather would use meat cases, cutting the thick glass to custom make tanks). So when I visited, I learned how to draw the outline of a fish by drawing two curvy lines that mirrored each other starting out by touching each other at the nose, then connecting the tail end with a single vertical line. Easy — three lines and you had drawn a fish!

Back at our elementary school, our art teacher taught us how to cut the large brick size gray blocks of clay to make the small tiles from — we literally made the tiles from scratch...hundreds of them. We baked, painted and glazed them — finally making a large 3' x 5' mosaic mural that still hangs inside the Cleveland Elementary School in Norwood. The final product is strongly reminiscent of ancient Roman murals from the 1st and 2nd centuries that are still being discovered by archaeologists today.

So, was this a "recognition memory"? Did the mere fact that I was involved in creating this mosaic in the same way that ancient Roman artists did 1800 years earlier, trigger in me some ancient memories of mosaics that I perhaps was surrounded by in a previous life?

The Catacombs

When I was 20 years old, as I previously mentioned, I studied in France on a Dartmouth foreign study program. I had never been to Europe before and since the $150 roundtrip airfare on Icelandic Airlines, while discounted, was still not cheap in 1971 dollars for a middle class family, I had planned ahead with two of my classmates to maximize that airfare expense. We decided to meet up, travel around Europe and see some sights as tourists before our semester started at the Université de Strasbourg.

We landed in Luxembourg, took a train to Paris and stayed with one of my classmate's family friends who was an executive at Air France. Every morning a case of tree-ripened Jaffa grapefruit was delivered to their doorstep fresh from Israel. I had never eaten grapefruit so sweet before. It required no sugar or honey!

Paris was awesome. It was just as I had imagined from watching 1950's movies at the drive-ins with my parents — *Funny Face* (1957) starring Audrey Hepburn and Fred Astaire... among others. We toured the city for several days and saw all the usual sites: the Louvre, Eiffel Tower, Versailles. Every night we had very comfortable accommodations in the Air France senior vice president's house — especially for three 20-year old, long-haired, hippie backpackers.

Then my friends suggested we take a train to see Rome, Italy. Both of them had been to Europe before, one even having lived in Paris. But I was a newbie, my first time in Europe. So, I said great, let's go check out Rome! After touring the Colosseum and other ancient sites in central Rome, we went to the catacombs along the Appian Way a few miles outside the main city.

Ancient Rome had been a walled city and bodies were not allowed to be buried within the city walls for sanitation reasons. So several miles outside the city were the catacombs, an underground labyrinth of tunnels and carved out rooms originally created and used by the Etruscans and Romans as mines, and later by the Jews and Christians to bury their dead.

When our taxi arrived, we saw 4-5 other tourists gathered in the parking area waiting for a tour to start. So our tour consisted simply of our small group of 7-8 of us and our tour guide holding a flashlight. We had to stay nearby him so as not to get lost in the pitch black darkness of the labyrinth of unlit tunnels, stairways and small rooms that stretched for 10 miles, up to 70 feet underground.

When we emerged from that underground world and resurfaced into the sunlight outside Saint Sebastian's church, I felt completely "out of it." I felt like I had been in another dimension, in a warped time-space continuum. I had no idea how much time had passed. You could have told me it was 5 minutes or an hour and 5 minutes, and I would have believed you. I actually asked my classmate and he checked his watch and said we had been down there for 25 minutes.

But the other really weird thing was: I *knew* I had been there before.

However, I had never flown on a jet airplane before this trip, never mind been in Italy or Rome before! Not this lifetime anyway.

So, that was my first "recognition memory" based on a place. The earlier ones I mentioned from the museums were based on artifacts.

I didn't yet know what lifetime or lifetimes I had been in those catacombs, but I knew I had been there before. I also had a similar feeling of "knowingness" and familiarity with the Colosseum and the Forum area in Rome.

All of those ancient "recognitions" began to surface on my European study abroad trip in Spring 1971. But little did I know at the time that it would only be the very beginning of recalling many more details of my having lived in Rome centuries earlier. I had just scratched the surface, had only just started to wipe away the dust that had collected on the surface of the mirror of my mind — for millennia.

Twenty years later starting in the 1990's, I began having memories of leading various battles and living daily life in ancient Rome as part of its aristocracy. This occurred sporadically for many years.

Catacombs, on the Appian Way outside of Rome

Gladiator

Then, when I saw the movie *Gladiator* in 1999, in an early scene when I saw Marcus Aurelius, I knew that I had been him. It was a "knowingness." There is no other way to explain this experience, other than a knowingness.

Similarly, how do I "know" that I am typing my book on a wireless keyboard now? Do I need to phone next door and ask my neighbor to come over and confirm with me what they see me doing? No. We just know what we are doing. Right?

In that same way, I knew at that moment that I had been Marcus. My soul, spirit, consciousness — my mind — was that same mind then as the mind that is in my current body now. Of course, it was a very different external life in the 2nd century, but the same internal mental experiencer then as the one now in the 21st century.

I did not know anything about Marcus Aurelius, other than he had been a Roman emperor. I had never studied anything about his life up to that point in my 20th century lifetime, nor had I ever read any of his writings.

After having that unusual experience while watching the movie *Gladiator* with my daughter Sam, I started researching information on him.

Years later when I finally got a copy of his famous collection of self reflections known as the "Meditations by Marcus Aurelius" in 2014, I was shocked by how similar our thoughts and writings were — his writings in the 2nd century and my writings in the 21st century. When I compared my writings and lectures from before I read his work, I could see the resemblance in thinking and often in even some of the maxims he and I are known for. For example, "control what you can control, and let go of what you can't control." I've been teaching that principle for the past 50 years. As it turns out, that is a classic Stoic principle that he wrote about that I was unaware of until recently.

Marcus Aurelius is known historically as a "philosopher-king." As emperor from 161-180 A.D., he led the Roman Empire which then accounted for approximately one-fifth of the world's population. He is considered one of the "Five Good Emperors" of Rome, known for his leadership as the last emperor of the *Pax Romana*, a period of relative peace and stability for the Empire. Marcus is also known to have been a great military leader of the Roman army, with the ability to think and plan strategically.

However, his primary personal interest was philosophy to which he devoted his lifelong study and practice. Marcus is known historically as one of the most widely respected Stoic philosophers. His philosophical pursuits, even while performing his duties later as emperor, inspired him to lead, as a practicing Stoic, what he called "a good life." He defined that as leading an ethical life, setting a healthy example for others, and thereby teaching them by demonstrating his views on virtues and life values in his personal and professional life. I have had many memories as Marcus ruminating on those concepts and explaining them to myself.

Interestingly, when Sam expressed great interest in going to see *Gladiator* with me, I was somewhat surprised. After all, she was only five years old at the time. She had seen the movie trailers, and was really excited to see the movie with me. It turns out that Sam also felt a deep affinity with ancient Rome and with the virtue displayed by the main character, the fictional Maximus played by Russell Crowe. Her recognition memories of having lived in ancient Rome began to resurface in her own consciousness after that.

Metropolitan Museum of Art

Starting in 2009 for several years I became a member of the Metropolitan Museum of Art in New York City for the primary purpose of visiting the Roman, Greek and Egyptian exhibits whenever I was in the city on business. One time I arrived, unaware of the museum hours, with only a short 15-minute window before the museum closed.

I was standing in the Greek and Roman section looking at some ancient armor, when suddenly my mind seemingly transported itself as if to a different time and place outside of the museum. I found myself unaware of my surroundings, yet deeply appreciating and feeling the "life" of that person who had worn that *cuirass* (armor that protects the torso from neck to waist, front and back) thousands of years ago. I remained standing immobile in that state of seeming suspended animation for I'm not sure how long.

Then, I was brought back to the present by the security guard's voice, when she said to me, "Excuse me...excuse me, sir, the museum is closed." She paused and continued, "It's very strange, because I didn't even see you standing there earlier, and I've been by here several times to clear the rooms."

Interestingly, I was in her direct, unobstructed line of sight standing only 20-25 feet away from her on the other side of the maroon velvet rope and stanchions that she had evidently put up across the exhibit entryway some time after I was standing there. There were no exhibits between her and me. Just open airspace.

Go figure.

It made me wonder if my mental experience had seemingly "convinced" her mind that I wasn't there so she couldn't see me (yet I suspect my image was still being picked up by the security system cameras).

Marcus Quotes

Ten years later starting around 2014, I began reading Marcus Aurelius quotes that I had been saying myself this lifetime in the 21st century to my classes without having read any of his maxims before.

Here is a sample of several quotes of his that I had unknowingly paraphrased or stated verbatim at various times over the past twenty years.

"It is not death that a man should fear, but he should fear never beginning to live."

"If someone is able to show me that what I think or do is not right, I will happily change, for I seek the truth, by which no one ever was truly harmed. Harmed is the person who continues in his self-deception and ignorance."

"Control what you can control. Let go of the rest."

But, the most surprising data point that seemed to "connect the dots" among several very unlikely events, places and personages came later in 2014 when I discovered the unusual and improbable relationship between Marcus Aurelius and a king of Prussia who lived and died 1600 years after the Roman emperor.

I will describe those details later when I recount that lifetime from the 1700's.

Chapter 11

Richard the Lionheart

1157-1199

Over the past 45 years, out of all my past lives, this 12th century lifetime has been the source of my most vivid and clear memories so far.

This was my second very clear past life memory. It happened on June 16, 1978 after receiving instruction in my fourth advanced TM technique from Lillian Rosen. I had just finished meditating with a half dozen friends at one of their parents' houses in Evanston, Illinois, and I was lying down resting afterwards. So I was not meditating, not sleeping, not dreaming, but I was in that wakeful resting state. Sometimes people call it that "twilight state" similar to right before you fall asleep.

Suddenly, it was as if my mind turned into a TV screen. I found myself standing alone in a large room, looking ahead as if through a camera — you know how sometimes in a dream you can see through your eyes but you can't see yourself? It was like that.

My vision was crystal clear as I paused and surveyed the whole room. I walked into this large stone room which appeared to be about 40 x 60 feet, made of huge blocks of stone — approximately two foot by three foot each. It had stone floors, high stone walls, and a stone ceiling, that as I turned my gaze upwards, I estimated was about 30-40 feet high.

I noticed there were no other people in the room. I was alone. And all of the furniture had been pushed against the walls, so the floor was clear...except for a large full-length mirror standing *by itself* in the middle of the room.

As I approached the large mirror, I saw my reflection begin to gradually fill it up, all the way to the edges of its wooden frame from top to bottom. So, standing there I knew I was a big guy, but at that point I didn't know exactly how big.

I was very tall with broad shoulders. I intuitively knew I was taller and larger than normal, even though there were no other people in the room to judge my size against. And I had long reddish hair and a red beard.

That was the first time I had ever seen myself as different looking — either in a dream or any other experience — other than what I recognized from 27 years at that point in this lifetime of being "Kelvin Chin."

I was wearing full-length chain mail from head to toe, and a large white tunic with a big red cross on it.

I was a crusader.

A split second later after I saw myself in the mirror — this whole experience probably happened very quickly in a matter of a few minutes — I knew that person in the mirror was me. I was looking at myself. The best way I can describe it is that I had the "knowingness" that was me.

And then, another split second later, doubt surfaced in my mind.

I had the feeling of "doubt" that it was me. But then a millisecond later, I experienced a very powerful jolt of energy that burst through my body from my feet all the way up through my torso into my head and shot out the top of my head. It was very powerful and similar in strength to the shock I felt as a teenager when I worked at a Boy Scout camp near Cape Cod. During a thunderstorm, we think a lightning bolt hit a tree near my building and its energy jumped onto the building into its rafters and through a nail I was hanging a metal saw onto.

That's how powerful the jolt of energy felt.

Along with that burst of energy in 1978 that shot through my body and out the crown of my skull came the experience once again of "knowingness" — the knowingness that I was in fact seeing myself in this experience.

The feeling went: "knowingness, doubt, knowingness" — all in a millisecond.

So, I relaxed and began to accept that experience for what it seemed to be. As I stopped resisting it and eased into more of an "allowing" mode, I began to remember experiences from this and many other lifetimes. The floodgates had opened.

In the Holy Land

For many months after that initial experience, during my meditations, I began to have clear visions of myself leading large armies of crusaders and slashing my broadsword on either side of myself on horseback, mowing down the enemy foot soldiers and sometimes engaging in hand-to-hand combat with black-bearded, darker skinned cavalry on horseback. I could even physically feel my sword going through the neck vertebrae and other body parts many times in many battles.

It was very tactile. In fact, all five senses were often activated as I began remembering experiences from that lifetime 800 years ago.

I could feel the weight of my sword and the strain on my shoulder, chest and back muscles — especially on my right side. And I could taste the dirt and dust of the battlefields as hundreds of horses churned up the desert in any given battle. I could feel the grit of blowing sand on my face and tiny grains of sand getting stuck in my teeth during those battles. I could smell the stench of sweat from the men and horses, and the putrid smell of rotting dead flesh, as well as the fetid, acrid odor of feces and vomit on the battlefields.

Over the decades since 1978, I've continued to have many of those experiences riding through dust on horseback with a four or five-pound broadsword, which is really heavy for a big sword. Most fighting swords in the 1100's were around two or three pounds.

Non-swordsmen often don't understand the physics and only look at the raw weight of a broadsword, which may sound fairly light. However, the length of the sword must also be taken into account. And swinging that much weight stretched out almost four feet requires great strength and stamina.

Many people mistakenly think broadswords were ten pounds or more. However, there is no way anyone could wield a sword that heavy, swinging it over and over hundreds of times throughout an entire battle.

Given how tall and strong Richard was, it is likely that he had one custom made on the heavier end of the spectrum to use in his battles, including in the crusades.

Anyway, I remember — viscerally — the enormous clouds of dust and the chaos in battle not only on horseback but other times on foot, wielding a smaller sword or battle ax while I was helmeted and wearing full mail armor wading through dense crowds of enemy infantrymen slicing a pathway through the sea of bodies. The dust of the desert battlefields, and the loud screaming and wailing of wounded and dying men is hard to forget.

I have very clear memories of fighting side-by-side with my cavalry and infantrymen, in the heat of battle and in some of the most crowded quarters, body-to-body, shoulder-to-shoulder, horse-to-horse.

The thunder of hundreds of hooves pounding on the ground from 1400-pound warhorses galloping at full speed while carrying their 200-300-pound fully armored crusader knights was deafening. The massive din was almost unbearable. There is no other way to describe it.

As horrific as it definitely was, it also yielded a somewhat euphoric and righteous feeling at times, especially given that many of us at the time believed that we were "doing God's work" by following the edict of the Pope to retake the holy city of Jerusalem from the Islamic leader Saladin and his troops. There was a feeling of great power seemingly invested in us by the Pope, the leader of Christianity.

I had many memories of being "in the zone" during battles where I could almost see what was going to happen before it happened, where everything around me — all of the chaos and loud noises — slowed down and was in slow motion...and at times silent. So, I became known as both a very skilled warrior on the battlefield in hand-to-hand combat, as well as a highly respected field general in the battle planning stage.

In the early 1980's, I also began having very clear recall of riding into battles leading my troops on horseback across desert landscapes. I was always at the phalanx of the crusader attack force on horseback, followed by thousands of troops on foot. It became something I was known for — putting myself at risk alongside my battle-hardened troops. And as I experienced, that became a source of loyalty among the troops nearly impossible to supplant.

In addition, I had many different memories living in castles, "feeling" the coldness and "seeing" the darkness inside these huge stone fortresses. I also have had many memories from that 12th century lifetime strategizing troop formations and planning their movement scenarios before battles in Europe.

For the past several thousand years, I have continued to be amazed at how poorly most battlefield commanders thought through their battle plans before they went into battle, and how many of them were just driven by their testosterone in their drive to win the battle at whatever cost, no matter how much their egos got in the way. It was often relatively easy to defeat those kinds of battlefield commanders because one could outthink them so effortlessly.

I was also — unfortunately for our enemies' troops — amazed at how cavalier and uncaring some generals were about the lives of their troops. As Richard, I clearly remember my concern for the well-being of my soldiers, both in terms of their physical health, as well as their battle preparation. Many of my 20,000 troops who were recruited to travel and fight in the Holy Land had little or no prior battlefield experience, so we knights had to train many of the foot soldiers in the basics of fighting and warfare — your basic "on-the-job training." Battle preparation also meant doing my part planning the battles as flawlessly as possible beforehand to ensure the highest probability of success.

In the Woods

Seemingly out of nowhere, I also started having memories from that lifetime being along the side of a road. And it was not in the Middle East, it was along a wooded road.

I was starving.

I saw myself, my lower torso and legs, eating a large animal — eating the flesh off of a huge 2-foot long, very thick bone. I ate it voraciously as if I had not eaten for many days. I could see many of my troops spread out in that wooded area, who were also devouring what probably had been one of our horses.

Perhaps one of our horses had died or maybe we sacrificed the horse so we wouldn't starve to death. All I knew for sure when I had this memory was that I was extremely hungry, and I had this huge shank of an animal bone with meat on it. And I was gnawing on the meat and bone.

Without a doubt, that's definitely not something that Kelvin Chin has ever done this lifetime...nor have I ever wanted to do. But in this experience, I had the visceral relief of avoiding starvation at that moment. A "visceral" feeling meaning that the incredible feeling of relief was almost overpowering. That feeling was impossible to ignore.

It was not the product of my regular thinking mind, from any "conscious thought" process. It seemed to be beyond the "controlling" part of my mind, an almost automatic feeling within my nervous system. It was as if it was "the only mental experience I could have at that moment," as I gnawed on the meat and bone.

Complete and utter emotional relief.

I think that's another data point. When I have these experiences that seem to be past life memories resurfacing, very often they are not just a visual experience. There's often a lot of emotion involved on a visceral level.

"Saracens"

In 2010, when I was living in Raleigh, North Carolina, I would often schedule business meetings in Los Angeles during which I would also spend "quality dad time" with my daughter Sam. She would stay with me in my hotel room, and I would take her to and from high school during my stays.

One morning, after we meditated together together in the Marriott Hotel at LAX, while I was lying down resting, I suddenly yelled out "Saracen swine!" repeatedly, and began swinging an invisible sword gripped by both hands. At the same time, I had visions of attacking on horseback with other helmeted crusaders wearing chain mail cloaked in white tunics with crosses, wielding swords cutting a swath through a crowd of dark-bearded foot soldiers.

After the meditation, Sam and I discussed what had just happened. She told me what I had been yelling and that I had been swinging my arms as if holding a sword. I had no recollection of either until Sam pointed that out to me. I evidently must have been so immersed in the experience that it had not registered in my conscious awareness.

Neither of us knew what the word "Saracen" meant. I didn't even know how to spell it correctly. So I looked it up on the internet, and discovered that it was the word for "Muslims" before the 1600's. I learned that "Muslims" was a relatively new term for the followers of Mohammed and the religion of Islam, and that during the Crusade in the 1100's, the term was "Saracens."

When I yelled out that word during my meditation, all I knew was that the emotion I was experiencing when I was shouting it was very intense, passionate and almost like yelling the more commonly heard battle cry, "Charge!" to my troops on horseback.

My Height and Weight

Starting in the late 1980's — about ten years after my first vision seeing myself standing in front of that large full length mirror — I had the knowingness of my exact height and weight from this lifetime. I was around 6'4" to 6'5" (195 cm), and about 225 to 230 pounds (104 kg). This came to me seemingly out of thin air. Although I still did not know the name of the person, I just somehow knew my body dimensions. These specific measurements just appeared in my mind one day and continued as a knowingness for many years afterwards.

Then twenty-five years later in 2014, a friend who knew of these past life experiences — including the one about knowing my height and weight, and hair color — asked me if I had ever read anything about the physical description of Richard the Lionheart, the king of England who led the Third Crusade in the late 1100's. And I said, "No."

He suggested that I look it up.

What I discovered was that Richard evidently was 6 foot 5 inches (195 cm) tall, of large stature, blue eyes with long red hair and a reddish beard, which was exactly how I saw myself in the experience I had in 1978. And then about ten years after that initial vision, I had added the knowingness of my height and weight.

That knowledge of my larger-than-normal bodily dimensions combined with the unusual color of my hair narrowed the field of possibilities of who I had been. There were not many human beings that large, and only 2% of the world's population was born with red hair. Those physical attributes along with the memory of being a leader of one of the crusades limited the names to one person: Richard the Lionheart.

Richard I ("Richard the First") has understandably been described as an imposing physical figure, a foot (or more) taller and 100-125 pounds heavier than the much shorter general male population in England of the 1100's, who averaged 5 foot 7 inches (170 cm) tall.

And one must remember, that when a human being is that much taller and heavier, *all* the body parts are much bigger — the head, shoulders, chest, arms, hands, legs and feet. I am 6'2" tall in my current lifetime and have taught meditation to professional basketball players who are just six to eight inches taller than I am, and yet I feel tiny standing next to them. They wore a size 17-18 shoe. I wear a size 12.

When I was Richard standing next to another man who was 12-15 inches shorter than I and 100-125 pounds lighter, the size differential was visually striking. Translating that to the battlefield, the power of my body fighting such a smaller opponent made it easy to overpower them in hand-to-hand combat. I wielded a sword often twice the weight of my opponents's weapon, thrusting it with my body which was 50% larger than his.

*Richard the Lionheart, Old Palace Yard outside
the Palace of Westminster, London*

That encapsulates the true meaning of the phrase "competitive advantage."

Richard was such an imposing figure at nearly 300 pounds when fully armed and helmeted on his 1400-pound (635 kg) warhorse, that there are documented first-hand accounts of his riding up one time to confront several hundred Saracens, who upon seeing how huge Richard was, turned around and ran away to avoid the fight.

Saladin

While his personal name was "Yusuf," he is generally known by the epithet "Saladin" (more accurately pronounced "Salah ad-Din"), an honorific that means "Righteousness of the Faith." Using that epithet, or descriptive phrase, would be the equivalent of calling Richard the Lionheart simply: "Lionheart."

In the late 1100's, Saladin quickly ascended the ranks of the Fatimid government in North Africa after his military successes against the early crusader assaults in the Middle East in and around Jerusalem.

Throughout the Third Crusade, Saladin and Richard's troops engaged in many battles in that region. The two men were very skilled military strategists and tacticians. And both had a shared desire to not waste the lives of their men unnecessarily, instead treating the lives of their men as critically important to their respective military and religious objectives.

My memories of both battling Saladin's troops as well as meeting with him several times to discuss a peaceful negotiated settlement are very clear and varied.

By the end of the Third Crusade, I grew to respect and understand Saladin as a great military mind and honorable leader of his people, and sought to end our conflict there, in as mutually beneficial a way as I could. Too many lives had been lost, and over what, I then asked myself.

I had begun to become disillusioned with the intentions of the Pope — what were his political motivations and how were they ostensibly linked to his alleged religious motivations, I wondered? I began to see — based on my experience on the ground in Jerusalem and the surrounding region — that those may have never been linked as closely as I had thought to any real "spiritual" objectives, but may have been a ruse to gain power for himself and to stop Christians from killing each other and to kill non-Christians instead. All of this killing, this "righteous" killing in the Holy Land, was not only sanctioned but ordered by the Pope...and by direct extension by God Himself, in God's name and under His orders. This led me to start to question his authority, as well as the concept of "spiritual authority" in general.

In retrospect, I think that may be why I started to explore other spiritual traditions in my subsequent lifetimes. The dogma of, in this case, Christianity no longer resonated with me, as I began to see fissures in the logic and dissonance in the Church's behavior. Their faith in a god seemed to be blinding even the highest levels of the Church from seeing their own greed and narcissism. If even they, who were personally invested by God with such "holy" power and insight, were corrupt, then what did that say about God himself, I asked myself?

Eleanor of Aquitaine

There is someone in my 20th century lifetime whom I think is one of the key reasons I chose to incarnate into the Chin family. My mother this lifetime.

In about 2018, I had the realization that she had been Eleanor of Aquitaine in the 1100's, married to Henry II, King of England. Thus, she was my mother when I was Richard I, and was responsible for grooming and positioning me for my ascension to the throne upon the death of my father Henry II.

For many decades, I had always known my mother was very different from other men and women of her generation, as well as within our maternal and paternal families. But it wasn't until I was quietly reflecting one day in 2018 about her life — her powerful and varied life — that it dawned on me about the ancient relationship that she and I shared.

She died tragically much too young in 1982 in her mid-50's. My mom was a true Renaissance woman. She could do almost anything she put her mind to. She was very intellectually intelligent, a chemistry major at Boston University, and socially gifted as the #1 salesperson for Fuller Brush in Massachusetts for a decade, as well as a talented creative artist expressed through her abstract painting, jewelry designs, and flowering rock gardens displayed in *Better Homes and Gardens*.

But what one noticed immediately — all of my childhood and college friends will attest to this — is that she commanded one's attention. She was only 5'0" tall, maybe 90 pounds, but she could command the room.

She had a powerful personality. An almost regal air. Appropriately, her Anglicized legal name, that she used her whole life since it sounded the closest to her Chinese given name, was "King." After she married my father, her name became:

King Chin

In my lifetime as Richard, my mother Eleanor raised me in the southwestern region of France called Aquitaine. Consequently, French was my native language which I spoke perfectly. In fact when I was later King of England, many commented on how poor my English was, yet how perfect both my French and Latin were. My facility with the latter was so compelling that it was written that "Richard's Latin was better than the Archbishop of Canterbury's."

But, back to my mother. As Eleanor, she groomed me starting when I was a child to be King of England, even though she had other sons who were in the hereditary line ahead of me. We are told that Richard was her favorite.

Interestingly, while political positions of authority are a part of my distant past, in this 20th century lifetime, as my mother King Chin, she continued her efforts to groom me for a successful life. When I was in kindergarten, she and I would take trips to downtown Boston to the bookstore where elementary school and high school teachers would buy their workbooks to supplement their textbooks for each subject. I can still picture the store sign — it was a black horizontal sign with gold lettering — but I cannot recall the name...it started with an H and had 2 M's...maybe Hammett or Hammell, I'm not sure. It was located somewhere on the streets behind the Parker House.

My mom would buy math and English workbooks for me. Each year in elementary school starting in kindergarten in 1956, she would give me assignments after school to study the material. Then I would sit at our kitchen table, she would turn the oven timer on, and I would do the timed quizzes and tests until I could do them within the allotted time frame and get all the answers right.

It was my mom's way of helping me get ahead of the classes by doing the work several weeks before the teachers assigned them. The teachers were well aware of what my mom was doing, as they discussed it openly together and coordinated with her on what assignments I was doing at home. But it's a good example of how committed my mom was to helping me succeed.

Here's another example:

In 2nd grade, my teacher gave the class an assignment to go home over the next few weeks, select a poem, memorize it and come back and recite the poem in front of the class. Most of the 7-year old kids went home and quite understandably picked a poem that had clear rhyming and repeating rhythmic patterns, and that, of course, were not too long — maybe 6-8 lines. One stanza.

What did I do?

Well, when my mom heard about this assignment (which I'm guessing she *already* knew about from the teacher before I'd even set foot back in our house that day after school), she suggested I memorize and recite the (I later found out) famous poem, "The Charge of the Light Brigade," an 1854 narrative poem by Alfred, Lord Tennyson about a battle in the Crimean War.

Tennyson was Poet Laureate of England and as such, was responsible for writing poems that captured important national events. Tennyson changed the poem up to 20 times before publishing it. The following is the first published version appearing in *The Examiner* on December 9, 1854 in London, less than two months after the events that inspired it took place at the Battle of Balaklava on October 25th. I copied the original which is on display in the British Library.

Picture a 7-year old boy standing in front of his 25 classmates reciting the following poem:

The Charge of the Light Brigade
By Alfred, Lord Tennyson

Half a league, half a league,
    Half a league onward,
All in the valley of Death
    Rode the six hundred.

Into the valley of Death
    Rode the six hundred,
For up came an order which
    Some one had blunder'd.
"Forward, the Light Brigade!
    "Take the guns," Nolan said:
Into the valley of Death
    Rode the six hundred.

"Forward, the Light Brigade!"
No man was there dismay'd,
Not tho' the soldier knew
    Some one had blunder'd:
Theirs not to make reply,
Theirs not to reason why,
Theirs but to do and die,
Into the valley of Death
    Rode the six hundred.

Cannon to right of them,
Cannon to left of them,
Cannon in front of them
    Volley'd and thunder'd;
Storm'd at with shot and shell,
Boldly they rode and well,
Into the jaws of Death,
Into the mouth of Hell
    Rode the six hundred.

Flash'd all their sabres bare
Flash'd all at once in air
Sabring the gunners there,
Charging an army, while
    All the world wonder'd:
Plunged in the battery smoke,
With many a desperate stroke
The Russian line they broke;
Then they rode back, but not
    Not the six hundred.

Cannon to right of them,
Cannon to left of them,
Cannon behind them
    Volley'd and thunder'd;

Storm'd at with shot and shell,
While horse and hero fell,
Those that had fought so well
Came from the jaws of Death,
Back from the mouth of Hell,
All that was left of them,
    Left of six hundred.

When can their glory fade?
O the wild charge they made!
    All the world wonder'd.
Honour the charge they made!
Honour the Light Brigade,
    Noble six hundred!

Battlefields

They are no fun.

If there is one takeaway from my past life memories I have recounted so far — especially this one as Richard the Lionheart because the crusader battlefield memories are so vivid for me — it is that war is not a playground. These are some of the most vivid sets of images that are seared into my memory banks — how ugly war is, how sad, how tragic, how utterly depraved it is.

It always amazes me how many people are at first "all in" on going to war, and then soon afterwards are often only "lukewarm" on it, then when their loved ones start dying and coming home in caskets, those same people frequently switch and become "against the war." I have observed this pattern of behavior worldwide for millennia.

I think if more of us had retained our memories of what the battlefields of war are really like, and not what Hollywood movies or TV ads from the military services themselves fantasize them to be, we would be more thoughtful and perhaps even more hesitant about jumping into wars so cavalierly. Thinking that anyone can "win" wars with "minimal" or "no casualties" is an illusion. And often it's stated as a boldface lie by politicians, most of whom have never had to kill another human being. I have seen this behavior first-hand for at least 2,000 years from Roman senators to their present day counterparts.

I am blessed or cursed, depending on how you look at it, with memories of thousands of years of fighting on the battlefields of Earth. What I recall most graphically are the battlefields strewn with dead or dying bodies, and the foul odor reeking of sweat, urine, feces, blood, and rotting flesh. It is very hard to describe but I can still almost "feel" viscerally the ugliness of all of that on my skin, and in my bones and muscles.

The memories of cradling my dead or dying brothers-in-arms are forever seared into my consciousness — as is my crying for them, for my loss of their lives. For my loss of our friendship. I feel that as if it were happening right now. And it does not matter if I believe in reincarnation — I miss them now.

After having had so much life experience on the battlefields, I decided to take a different direction in my several subsequent lifetimes, and I chose to instead "turn within."

Chapter 12

The Monastic Period

1200-1700

I have memories of several lifetimes as a monk, and a couple of what I would call "more inward-facing" almost monastic lives sandwiched between some of those lives as an actual Buddhist monk. It was a series of lifetimes where I seemed to be spending more time searching inward, within myself, exploring the inner reaches of my individual consciousness as well as my thinking and beliefs, and less time on the effects I could have realizing accomplishments in the outer world around me. Thus, I call this period of my lifetimes, my "monastic period."

My memories of these lifetimes during this period are not as detailed as many of my others. It's as if the "jigsaw puzzle pieces" (memories) are there, but not as many are readily accessible. However, there are some pieces of the puzzle that give some interesting insights into both how my mind and personality has persisted throughout the 6,000 years, and how I think we can make many different choices in our journeys.

Buddhist Monk in Tibet

After my crusader lifetime, where I followed the Pope's mandate to try to retake Jerusalem from the Saracens, which proved in the end to be unsuccessful, I chose while I was on the Other Side between lives to take a different approach to life. I rethought my approach to religion and decided on taking a different path, and I incarnated in Tibet and pursued a life as a Buddhist monk.

I was a serious student of Buddhism in the Tibetan tradition. I lived in a community of other monks where we immersed ourselves in Buddhist teachings.

Buddhist Monk in China

After spending some time on the Other Side between lifetimes, I came back fairly soon again, this time as a Buddhist monk somewhere in China to continue my introspective work but in a biological body. In this lifetime, in addition to long periods of solitude, contemplation and meditation, I eventually became a teaching monk.

I had a number of students at the time, some of whom have reconnected with me and reincarnated as friends and family in later lifetimes, including this one during the 20th century.

I have had experiences during or after my meditations over the decades from the 1980's to the present where I will speak in what sounds like it might be a form of classical Chinese that I recognize from my graduate school studies at Yale. I think that may be related to this lifetime.

Muslim Son of Maharishi Mahesh Yogi, before 1592

I am not exactly sure what years this lifetime occurred. However, it must have been before 1592 when Maharishi Mahesh Yogi (his 20th century name) incarnated as Shah Jahan because I was not part of his family during that lifetime. Jahan was the 16th century Mughal emperor and builder of the famous Taj Mahal in India.

During the run-up to the 30th November 2014 event I was organizing, in one of my meditations the group known as "the Movement" came to me telepathically to give me some instructions about the meeting logistics and lighting, how many cameras to have to record the event and why, etc.

The event was a series of explanations that were given to George Hammond during a series of conversations in January 2014 by some of the founders of the Judeo-Christian-Islamic-Vedic traditions. There were about 15-20 of them who came to George, as well as several others and me, to share information they wanted to have disseminated at this 30th November event that was held in Alexandria, Virginia (https://www.30thNovember.com).

But, as I said, during one of my regular twice daily meditation sessions, members of that group came to discuss some things with me. And at the end of that discussion about meeting logistics, one of them paused and said, "Oh, and Maharishi wants us to tell you that you were his son in another lifetime."

My immediate thought was, "What? I thought he was a monk the whole time, never a householder (someone who raised a family)."

Over the subsequent two weeks or so after that message, I started having memories of his being my father in a Muslim lifetime. And in particular, I distinctly recalled his being a difficult father — that he loved me, but that he could be harsh, righteous and unforgiving of my mistakes. And moreover, that he had very high expectations of how he wanted me to display and express my spiritual side —something that I rebelled against vehemently.

I sought to be a spiritual person, but in my own way. Not his way.

I recall that we lived in a Muslim culture and were of the upper class. And I had a harem of women. This series of memories of that lifetime all quickly popped up in my awareness in 2014 while I was sitting quietly one day in my apartment in Austin, Texas.

One very clear memory I have is walking into a building in an arid, hot region in the Middle East. It was my home where I lived with my family. I recall it was about midday (I could tell by the angle of the sunlight and feel of the heat).

Up on the second floor, I recall striding confidently into a large room with a sense of purpose (I do not recall why). I had a harem, which was not uncommon in that culture at that time. In this room, all of my wives and concubines were relaxing and chatting — about a dozen were sitting and reclining there, dressed in very lightweight, gossamer, gauze-like, flowing clothing.

I had a favorite, one with whom I felt the closest, and I saw her get up, and run to greet and embrace me. We chatted. I also remember she was the "head of the household" — the apparent manager of all these women.

In that Muslim lifetime, she was highly respected and revered by the other women in my harem. She ruled as if she were my queen without the formal title. Emotionally, she felt like my primary wife.

I recall today who she was then. And interestingly, I recall who she was 2,000 years ago when we were with Jesus.

But what is perhaps even more interesting is that my father knew her, and knew her well. He was the same soul or personality who would later incarnate and be known as Maharishi Mahesh Yogi in the 20th century, with whom I studied in the 1970's and with whom this friend's life story 2,000 years ago would have overlapped if John the Baptist (another previous lifetime of Maharishi) had not been beheaded.

This highlights how in a number of my lifetimes I have noticed that many of us can and do overlap and meet each other, and may interact once again in varying relationships over the millennia. This example also shines a light on the fact, which I've witnessed so many times over the past 6,000 years, that sometimes unforeseen circumstances can intervene, based on the choices of people we may not even know, that may derail what otherwise would be meaningful connections and relationships.

Buddhist Monk in Southeast Asia

In the 1980's, I had this memory of being a monk in Southeast Asia. The very clear visual and visceral experience I recall was sitting cross-legged in meditation with a group of monks, and occasionally getting energy rushes through my body that would cause me to hop or jolt my body in such a way that I was bouncing on the straw mats we were sitting on.

I am not exactly sure when this lifetime occurred, but my sense is that it may have been sometime in the 1500's.

The following "knowingness" is something that surfaced in my awareness within the past several years: that I sometimes chose to be a monk primarily for the solitude, not so much for the specifics of the spiritual tradition associated with that lifetime.

I sometimes viewed choosing lifetimes as a monk to be a good alternative to living on the Other Side in an energy body, yet still being able to have my "alone time." Being a monk was a way to enjoy physical reality and a biological body, without as many of the challenges of having to take care of that body — which typically requires a job to make money for food, shelter, and other basics.

It was a way to have a physical biological body while being "on vacation." Meaning, I was being taken care of by the monastic order with decent food and simple shelter.

Often in my monastic lifetimes, I just "did my own thing" and enjoyed being left alone to contemplate my ideas, while doing whatever basic responsibilities I had to perform for the monastery. But for the most part, I was often left alone to be in my room in solitude. Sometimes that was an actual part of the structure of our monastic life and other times I would somehow arrange for that extra alone time for myself regardless of the formal structure of that particular monastery.

I wasn't always in that mindset during each of my lives as a monk. As I already said, there were monastic lifetimes, or periods within them, where I was a teacher sometimes with many students, some of whom I seem to have stayed connected with from lifetime to lifetime.

But I found this epiphany about why I found monastic life to be a desirable choice an interesting one. It surprised me at first. Then again, knowing myself as I do, upon further reflection, it seemed to fit my personality quite aptly.

Samurai, Japan, 1600's

In 2009, I started having experiences during meditation where I would speak in Japanese and move my arms as if

I was wielding an invisible sword. When I say "wield a sword," I would involuntarily and spontaneously start seeing visions of battles, and much like with my crusader memories, my muscle memory in my mind and body would cause slashing and stabbing movements with my shoulders and arms. It would feel as if I was in battle.

This first started happening in a hotel room on my business trips back to Los Angeles, when I was visiting with my daughter who was then still in high school there. Keep in mind that my kids have grown up since birth meditating with their father who has occasionally done this unusual stuff, so by the time Sam was a teenager she found these additional "extracurricular meditation movements" by her dad not merely normal, but extremely amusing. In fact, Sam would often ask me when she was three-years old if she could sit on my lap when I meditated so she could "go for a ride" because I would sometimes move and bounce my legs involuntarily and blurt out stuff, sometimes in English, sometimes in other languages.

In addition, occasionally in my quiet moments as I am getting ready to meditate, as well as during or after my meditations, I have spoken in what sounds like Japanese.

I did study Japanese as a required second East Asian language as part of my graduate program when I was a PhD candidate at Yale in the East Asian Languages and Literatures program. However, I only took a year of that language and was not fluent enough to remember very much dialogue or vocabulary.

That said, I do know what it sounds like and how to pronounce the language. So when this spontaneously happens in those quiet moments, it definitely sounds like I am speaking Japanese. And moreover, the emotional force with which I say certain things aligns with the visuals I have with my samurai activities.

I don't have a lot of specifics from that lifetime in Japan, and I am not sure of the exact dates of this lifetime. But I have clear memories of training and fighting as a samurai.

However, I also have memories of introspection in that lifetime as a samurai — where I was "turned within" contemplating life, ideas, and ontological concepts. In addition, I have the sense that I had some leadership role administratively when I was a samurai. Those elements have led me to think that this lifetime was closer to the end of the samurai era when there was less fighting going on compared to its earlier days in the 1300's.

And since I am fairly certain who I was in my lifetime in the 1700's, this Japanese one must have happened before then, most likely in the mid to late 1600's. My memories would therefore fit with the changes in the role of the samurai which were occurring during that period.

Chapter 13

Frederick the Great

1712-1786

"A King of Prussia"

In 1979, I first had the "knowingness" that I had been "a king of Prussia." Again, I cannot explain why I knew that, but I just did. It was as clear as day, as the saying goes. And it came out of nowhere as part of that flood of past life memories that spontaneously gushed forth from within me from time to time, starting in late 1977.

For at least 40 years, I have "known" that I had been *a king* in Prussia. I didn't know for the first several decades any more than that. And, quite frankly, I was not moved to look into it any further because back in the 1970's to 1980's the only person I shared these memories with was my good friend George Hammond, whom we had figured out had been my brother 2,000 years ago. He and I had decided that there was no particular reason to tell anyone else, because we didn't have any plans to do anything with these memories. So, we kept them private between ourselves.

Consequently, I just parked that knowingness that I had "been a king in some place called Prussia at some point in the distant past." I didn't even bother to research where exactly Prussia was, or when it existed, although I did have a sense that it had something to do with Germany, so I knew it must have been a place in Europe. My book knowledge of history was not very deep. Even when I was in high school, I did not elect to take the European History course that most of the kids took. I only took U.S. History, which was required to graduate. As a result, I had no idea during what time period in history this place called Prussia existed.

Over the subsequent years, I started having more memories surfacing that seemed to relate to that Prussian lifetime. For example, I would get flashes of scenes in castles and ballrooms, of meetings and dances and period music, as well as clothing and women with their hair coiffed in styles that seemed to be from the 18th century. I was somewhat familiar with the clothing from that era having acted in several French plays while I was a student at Dartmouth College, in particular some works by Voltaire, including some scenes from his famous novel, *Candide*.

For some reason, that my memories were from a place called "Prussia" continued to be very clear in my mind, although the details of the lifetime did not become clear to me until fairly recently in 2014. That was thirty-five years after the first inkling surfaced.

Which King of Prussia

My curiosity was piqued in the summer of 2014, when I read something unusual in a biography about Marcus Aurelius. I was living in Austin, Texas at the time working for a legal services company.

I had gone to the local library branch one weekend several blocks from my apartment and was perusing the biographies along the aisle pertaining to Marcus Aurelius. One in particular caught my eye…or my attention actually…a book researched and written by a British historian named Frank McLynn. As I thumbed through several chapters, while standing in the stacks at the library, I noted that McLynn seemed objective and without any hidden agenda — political, religious, or otherwise — in his writing about Marcus. This attracted me as I was seeking the most objective views on Marcus. McLynn seemed to be drawing his research material from sources that he had vetted as reliable, for what seemed to be clear and logical reasons. As I read some of his material, the substance of McLynn's writing also intuitively just "felt accurate." So for all those reasons, I decided to check the book out from the library.

Several days later at home, when I got to page 508, a phrase on the page jumped out at me.

In this chapter buried near the end of the book, McLynn was talking about people through history who had revered, respected and spoken highly of Marcus Aurelius, the 2nd century Roman emperor. As I read about an 18th century widespread fascination with the concept of the "philosopher-king," the book said that "Pope Benedict XV was hailed by his supporters as one such figure, and even stronger claims were adduced for Frederick the Great of Prussia, a man who consciously modeled himself on Marcus Aurelius."

I nearly dropped the book on the floor. The phrase I had just read was: "who consciously modeled himself on Marcus Aurelius."

Who was this guy? Was he *that* king of Prussia?

I looked him up. Sure enough. Yes, he was. Frederick II, King of Prussia, was affectionately called Frederick "the Great" by his citizenry.

As I read further in that chapter, McLynn again revisited what he considered one of Marcus Aurelius's most intriguing traits — that of the philosopher-king. And once again, McLynn cited Frederick the Great as the 18th century's candidate for philosopher-king, reiterating that he "expressly modeled himself on Marcus," *who preceded him by 1600 years.*

Moreover, Frederick surrounded himself with other philosophers, most notably Voltaire. In addition, according to McLynn, Frederick's 1739 work the *Anti-Machiavel* "was meant to be in the Aurelian idiom." In that work, Frederick attacked Machiavelli, author of *The Prince*, for his advocacy of scorched-earth policies (murder, plunder, etc.), among other things.

Antoninus

In addition, McLynn informs us that Frederick sought out and purchased a beautiful and expensive 2nd century statue sculpted in the Antonine period, and placed it prominently in a wooded grove at his favorite palace, *Sanssouci,* in Potsdam near Berlin.

What is the significance of that?

Antoninus Pius was the Roman emperor who preceded Marcus Aurelius, and who succeeded Hadrian. Marcus's father died when he was three years old. Soon thereafter, the emperor Hadrian took a liking to Marcus and began grooming him to be emperor of Rome—with the intent of adopting him when Marcus was older. For example, when Marcus was just 6 years old, the emperor promoted the young boy to the equestrian (knight) class. When Marcus was 8 years old, Hadrian enrolled him as one of the twelve Salii priests, all patrician youths, in the Salii college where he performed rituals and participated in religious parades. This was Hadrian's way of getting young Marcus "seen" by the public in leadership roles arising from these state-sponsored rituals that were considered important for the maintenance of the Roman social order. But when Hadrian was on his deathbed, because Marcus was still too young (17 years old), Hadrian had to come up with an alternate plan. To create a "bridge" for Marcus until he was older, the emperor Hadrian adopted Antoninus who was married to Hadrian's niece. Antoninus was in his early 50's.

However, as a condition of Antoninus's adoption to become Hadrian's adoptive son and therefore immediate heir to the throne, he arranged for Antoninus to also adopt Marcus, so that Hadrian was assured that Marcus would ascend to the throne at some point after his (Hadrian's) death. Hadrian died within a month afterwards.

Hadrian chose Antoninus not only because he thought he would be a good emperor, but also because at 52 years old, Antoninus was not expected to live too much longer, several years at most. So by then, Marcus in his mid-20's would be a perfect age to become emperor of Rome.

At least that's what Hadrian was guessing would happen. However, Antoninus had an exceptionally strong physical constitution, and lived for another 22 years dying at age 74, which is why Marcus did not become emperor until age 40.

Notwithstanding that elaborate succession plan, according to Marcus's own writings as well as those of contemporary historians, Marcus Aurelius was very close to his stepfather Antoninus Pius. He loved him dearly. And Marcus greatly respected and learned a lot from observing Antoninus's measured leadership skills.

So, could it be that Frederick the Great who may have been Marcus Aurelius in a previous lifetime 1600 years earlier still had a subconscious or perhaps even conscious emotional connection with the relatively unknown Roman emperor Antoninus Pius, who just so happened to have been Marcus's stepfather and predecessor emperor? And consequently, could that have been the reason that Frederick sought out that expensive 2nd century Roman statue sculpted during the Antonine era to display prominently at his palace, *Sanssouci*, in Prussia in the mid-18th century?

We will never know for sure. But it is food for thought.

Wilhelmine

Sometime in 2016, when my daughter Sam was a senior at San Francisco State University, something unusual happened while I was telling a story to one of my clients about her. I mistakenly said, "My sister...I mean my daughter, is a dance major at SFSU."

I had made a similar verbal slip-up like that more than a dozen times over the previous several years even while she was in high school. I never said anything to Sam about that, figuring it was just one of those "dad slip-ups" that we all do occasionally.

Then one day right before I was going to call Sam to discuss planning a visit to come see one of her dance performances, it happened again. So when I phoned her a few minutes later, I casually mentioned that most recent incident. And, to my surprise, she said excitedly, "Dad, you won't believe it, but I've been slipping up for years calling you my brother! Like when

I tell my friends that you teach meditation, sometimes I'll say, 'My brother...I mean my dad, teaches meditation....' I just never told you!"

The order of the following events related to this realization that she and I "may have been sister and brother" in another lifetime happened as follows. At this point, we did not know which lifetime.

First, we stumbled by accident on the realization that mutually — for many years, at least five years — we had been slipping up in our stories about the other person when we were simply conversing with friends, acquaintances or work colleagues, calling the other person incorrectly "my brother" or "my sister." Neither of us had said anything to each other about those slip-ups prior to about 2016.

Then, in 2019 which was three years after the realization of those slip-ups — still with no connecting the dots to any particular lifetime — Sam got signed by the global modeling agency, Wilhelmina Models, headquartered in New York City.

While I had first realized I had been Frederick in 2014, it was subsequent to Sam's signing with Wilhelmina Models in 2019 that I had a memory of "losing my sister" when I had been Frederick. At that point, I did not know that sister's name or any details other than I just had the very strong emotional knowingness that we had been very close as "a brother and sister."

So, I decided to research if Frederick had any siblings. I discovered that he did.

He had six sisters and three younger brothers. He was closest to his eldest sister. She was three years older than Frederick. They had an extremely close relationship from childhood, throughout their entire adult lives. Emotionally, she was his closest sibling.

When she died fairly young in her late 40's, approximately 30 years before Frederick's demise, he reportedly went into a deep depression for several weeks. There are many accounts of how overwhelmed he was by the grief of his sister's death.

To help him process his grief by expressing his love for her, Frederick built a beautiful, Corinthian-columned domed structure, reminiscent of ancient Rome, commemorating her life. He called it the "Temple of Friendship." It sits in the garden behind Frederick's palace of *Sanssouci* in Potsdam, and is a tribute to his favorite sister at his favorite palace.

Some time after learning that he in fact had been very close to his eldest sister, I had the knowingness that my daughter this lifetime had been my sister in that lifetime. But at that point when I had that knowingness of Sam being that sister, I still did not know her name.

What was Frederick's eldest sister's name?

Wilhelmine

We had reunited *again* in the 1700's. I say "again," because she had been my daughter 1,700 years earlier in my Simon Peter lifetime.

Now, you might think I would have seen the odd connection between Frederick's sister's name and my daughter Sam's modeling agency, but nope. My friend, George Hammond, had to point that out to me! I guess I was so immersed in the emotion and realization that Sam and I had been that particular brother and sister that I had not noticed the Wilhelmine/ Wilhelmina connection.

So, my daughter Sam this lifetime was my eldest sister Wilhelmine when I was Frederick II of Prussia.

Interestingly, in 2019 she submitted to eight different modeling agencies — this was her fourth round of sending in her measurements and digitals to these same agencies. The only one that responded to her was Wilhelmina Models. And they signed her immediately to a multi-year contract.

Could her friends on the Other Side have whispered to the agents there to open her submission form this time?

More food for thought.

Temple of Friendship – built by Frederick in honor of his sister Wilhelmine at Sanssouci, Potsdam

The Brochure

Another interesting "coincidence" occurred in August 2019.

Earlier that year, I had received an email from a woman who was helping to organize speakers for the IANDS (International Association for Near Death Studies) annual conference. When she phoned me, she told me she had "prayed to God asking to be guided to someone whom she should invite to speak at this conference, someone who would give a different perspective to the material about NDE's and the Afterlife." She said her prayers were answered and she had been directed to contact me.

She encouraged me to submit some ideas of topics I could speak on, and several of them were accepted. About a month before the conference, she asked me if I had a brochure that described the various classes I taught, as well as a description of my book. I replied, No. She strongly suggested that I create one, so it could be included in all the conference bags that each of the 500 registrants would receive.

So, I got busy gathering the material for a brochure.

However, I am not a design person. So when my friend told me that she had her brochure done by Vistaprint and that for an extra $20 you could get a graphic designer to design your brochure, I was all in.

I went online and uploaded all of my content to their website, including photos for my brochure. The graphic designer then sent me the draft brochure. He independently had decided on the placement of the various classes on the six panels, and picked the different colors and fonts. I liked it, told him a few edits, and signed off on it.

A few minutes later after hanging up, I was in my kitchen washing my breakfast dishes when I got a "whisper" from the Other Side: "It's Prussian blue, you know."

I thought, "Huh? What's Prussian blue? Is that a real name of a color?"

So I immediately went to my laptop, typed in "Prussian blue" into the internet browser, and…what I discovered was that the name Prussian blue originated in the beginning of the 18th century, when the compound was used to dye the uniform coats for the Prussian Army. Prussian blue was the predominant color of the coats worn by the cavalry, infantry and artillery regiments of the Prussian Army.

The graphic designer had chosen Prussian blue for my brochures. Had he been "whispered" to by my friends on the Other Side, perhaps some of my former soldiers from the Prussian Army in the 1700's? I don't know.

And when I researched the color of the Prussian Army's uniforms further, I discovered that the burnt orange-almost gold color of the piping and around the buttonholes of the coats and pants also matched the borders around the photos on my brochure, as well as the headings on each of the six panels.

When I told my friend George Hammond about this highly unusual series of "coincidences" relating to my brochure, he said, "Well, you know there's a joke going on over on the Other Side among our friends, don't you?" I said, "What are you talking about?" George said, "Well, look where the conference is being held."

Even though I had been asked and approved several months earlier in the Spring to speak at the August/September IANDS Conference, I had not made the connection between its location that year and the fact that it was the first time I would speak publicly at any conference about my lifetime as Frederick the Great. It was being held in King of Prussia, Pennsylvania.

It turns out that not only is the town named "King of Prussia," but it also was named specifically in honor of Frederick the Great. In 1719, Welsh Quakers established a farmhouse that was later converted to a tavern and inn, which became the "The King of Prussia Inn" in 1769. It was so named by the owner to honor the 18th century Prussian monarch Frederick the Great, who opposed Britain's imperial ambitions. Given the ideal location of the inn at a crossroads exactly one day's travel from Philadelphia by horse, and later the location of a railway station, by 1850 the township had also adopted the same name as the inn.

When I shared this with George, he laughed and said, "Our friends [on the Other Side] have been planning this 'coming out' party for you!"

The William Baldridge and Charlie Lutes Story

How close can we get to "really knowing" if these past life memories are real and not a product of our imagination?

This recent 2020 series of events surprised even me. Here is what happened.

I have taught an "Afterlife & Reincarnation" series since 2018, about three times a year. In January 2020, I became Facebook friends with someone named William Baldridge. Coincidentally, we had both taught Transcendental Meditation (TM) in the 1970's but had never crossed paths back then, since he was on the West Coast in California, and I was teaching on the East Coast in New England, New York, and then later in Asia.

In February 2020 he took my Afterlife & Reincarnation series, so he heard my story of how my past life memories first resurfaced in 1977. After the session on reincarnation, William ("Widge") and I were chatting on the phone — he was intrigued in particular by my memory of being Simon Peter.

Then, he told me this story.

When Widge was a college student studying at Maharishi International University (MIU) in 1973, soon after its founding — when they were still renting some buildings to use as dormitories and classrooms in Goleta, a city in southern Santa Barbara County, California — a group of students would regularly drive down to Los Angeles to hear the weekly lectures given by a TM teacher named Charlie Lutes. I did not know Charlie Lutes, but I had heard in the 1970's that he was one of the first people to have met Maharishi Mahesh Yogi and to have learned meditation from him when that guru came to the U.S. from India in 1959. Charlie Lutes, already a successful businessman in his 50's, was trained by Maharishi to teach his meditation technique in the 1960's.

I had also learned through hallway conversations in the local TM centers when I was teaching meditation on the East Coast that Charlie Lutes was head of another arm of the TM organization called the Spiritual Regeneration Movement (SRM) headquartered on the West Coast. As the name implied, SRM was more into promoting the spiritual benefits of meditation and so it appealed to audiences interested in those topics. I had no contact with SRM. Their focus did not interest me.

In fact, the leaders of the TM organization I was involved in — International Meditation Society (IMS), Students International Meditation Society (SIMS) and Institute for Fitness and Athletic Excellence (IFAE) — advised us to keep our distance from the SRM folks, and especially its leader, Charlie Lutes. The reason was that we were focusing our outreach and teaching efforts on businesses, educational institutions, prisons, and sports teams. And we figured the last thing any of those industry leaders wanted to hear about was "woo-woo" stuff like "spirituality." Our target audiences were solely interested in stress reduction and increasing productivity. That's what we focused on when we spoke about meditation.

Moreover, we were very sensitive and cognizant of not appearing like a religion, any more than something called "meditation" coming out of a Hindu country like India already did. In the 1970's — unlike today — meditation was considered "foreign" to the Western world and was viewed with suspicion by the masses and the media. What SRM and Charlie Lutes were doing, we felt, fit right into that negative stereotype that the masses in the U.S. automatically assumed when they heard the word "meditation." Consequently, we avoided him and his lectures about spirituality.

Furthermore, on a personal level, we who were teaching meditation to the business, education and sports communities didn't even believe in the stuff that Charlie Lutes and his wing of the organization were talking about. "Reincarnation — what, wait? Are you serious? Do you really believe in that *past lives* stuff?" That was the reaction we had in our arm of the organization.

So, back to the story Widge told me in 2020.

Evidently, on one of those trips to hear Charlie Lutes speak in Los Angeles in the Fall of 1973, several of those MIU students reported that they had heard an audience member ask Charlie specific questions about reincarnation, concerning people who were around Jesus when Jesus was alive.

Widge told me: "To my great surprise, my friends reported that Charlie Lutes said that some of the personalities around

Jesus back then are alive again today, and are associated with the TM organization. To my greater surprise, they said Mr. Lutes cited an example of one such individual who had lived and worked with Jesus while Jesus was on Earth, Simon Peter also known as Saint Peter. He went on to say that this same soul had other significant lifetimes, plural, including one as a very great military and political leader, Frederick the Great. And that he was currently a TM teacher in the TM organization."

After Widge told me this, I asked him to go back and check with some of his friends who heard this first-hand from Charlie Lutes at that lecture back in 1973. He checked with them and they confirmed that his recollection of that story was accurate.

Moreover, this story from Widge and his friends that arose from the lecture by Charlie Lutes occurred in the Fall of 1973. It was not until the Fall of 1977 that *any* of my past life memories began to resurface — four years after this lecture in Los Angeles by Charlie Lutes.

In addition, while the general knowingness that I had been a king of Prussia appeared in my consciousness in 1979, it wasn't until 2014 — a full 41 years after the statement by Charlie Lutes in his lecture — that I recalled *which* king of Prussia I had been.

According to Widge and his friends, in Fall 1973 Charlie Lutes made the statement that this reincarnated personality was also a TM teacher. Interestingly, I had completed my teacher certification with Maharishi six months earlier in Spring 1973.

Prior to Widge recounting this series of events, I had never met Charlie Lutes nor heard any of his lectures or stories about them. The TM teachers on the East Coast were explicitly instructed by our regional director to avoid everything associated with Charlie Lutes. And we did.

That story that William Baldridge shared with me in 2020 is by far the most unlikely third-party corroboration I have received so far concerning any of my past life memories.

Here is a letter from William Baldridge describing the series of events in even greater detail:

The William G.G. Baldridge Letter

To Whom It May Concern:

In 1973 in Santa Barbara California, then the home of Maharishi International University, some of my friends would drive down to L.A. for once-a-week lectures on TM by the head of the Spiritual Regeneration Movement, which was a TM-related organization. Unlike Maharishi Mahesh Yogi, Charlie Lutes would answer questions from meditators regarding a wide range of topics, such as angels, heaven, and reincarnation.

Returning to Santa Barbara following one of those weekly lectures, my friends reported that someone had asked specific questions about reincarnation concerning the individuals who were around Jesus when Jesus was alive. To my great surprise, my friends reported that Charlie Lutes said that some of the personalities around Jesus then are alive again today and are associated with the TM organization. To my even greater surprise, Mr. Lutes cited an example of one such individual who had lived and worked with Jesus while Jesus was on Earth, Simon Peter also known as Saint Peter. This surprised me a great deal, so I never forgot about it. One reason it surprised me is that traditional Hindu dogma held that saints would very rarely incarnate again. However what Mr. Lutes said was that not only is Saint Peter among us today in the TM organization but that this personality or soul had also lived other significant lifetimes, including as the very great political and military ruler, Frederick the Great. Again, it was shocking for me as a Christian to hear that someone as presumably spiritually advanced as Saint Peter, has had any subsequent lives, much less one as a military and political leader.

So, from 1973 until the present, a small number of us had learned from Charlie Lutes, who remains a very reliable source on such matters, that Saint Peter had also lived a life as Frederick the Great and was currently a TM teacher in the TM organization. By the way, in February of 2020 I went back and checked with my longtime friend from those days in college, James R. of Arkansas, to confirm that my memory of all these matters back in 1973 was correct. James remembered the details the same way I do. From that point in 1973 onward, I had just assumed that the individual in question knew well who he was and simply wished to keep his identity from being known publicly or even inside the TM organization. So it was with great surprise that I discovered that this individual, who was indeed a TM teacher in the TM organization back in 1973 had not known of his past life as Simon Peter until 1977, nor had he any intimation of his life as Frederick the Great until 1979, and indeed is today Kelvin Chin.

Conversely, Kelvin Chin was surprised to learn that a handful of other MIU students and I in Santa Barbara had been aware since 1973 of the fact that St. Peter and Frederick the Great were but two separate lifetimes of an individual who, like the rest of us, had become a TM teacher. Kelvin had not determined which Prussian king he had been until late 2014.

William Baldridge

William G.G. Baldridge
February 20, 2023

*Kelvin Chin with Maharishi Mahesh Yogi, TM Teacher
Training Course, La Antilla, Spain, May 13, 1973*

Chapter 14

Eagle

I am unsure when this lifetime occurred but I know it occurred sometime after my Buddhist lifetimes and before my next lifetime. So, I am placing it here in the chronology for those reasons, along with the fact that my next lifetime revered and respected eagles for what they symbolized in that culture.

This memory resurfaced in my awareness on April 4, 2020. It happened after one of my meditations with one of my "Turning Within" Meditation students, while I was lying down in the rest period afterwards. So, I was in that "in between" state — not meditating, not wide awake, not dreaming, and not sleeping. I was aware but somewhat mentally floating from thought to thought without focusing, quite like during my meditations, but in more of an observer mode at that point in my rest period.

In this experience, I had the very clear vision and visceral sense of flying. At that point in the beginning of the experience I was simply looking out of my own eyes and was having the explicit experience of soaring on the air currents above a wooded area of what appeared to be evergreen trees for as far as I could see in all directions. I estimated that I was thousands of feet above the forest below. I could see mountains in the distance, some snow covered with a carpeting of forestation between them and me. I was riding the thermals over a very hilly wooded area with occasional rock cliffs.

The air was cool but not cold. Refreshing. Clean and clear. I saw no buildings or any sign of human habitation anywhere — no roads, no structures, no smoke. It felt to me like I was somewhere in the Pacific Northwest, maybe even farther north towards what we now call Alaska.

I adjusted my wings that I could now see stretched out on either side of me, and that adjustment caused me to fly gradually down towards the treetops, then faster and faster, skimming along the treetops maybe 20-30 feet from them, then rising back up riding a thermal higher and higher soaring to about 1,000 feet.

Then at that point in the experience I had an "experience within the experience" so to speak. I started having some memories of experiences I had had in that lifetime — of eating animals that I had caught.

It was one of those 3-dimensional experiences that I had had many times in my rest period after meditations. It felt totally real, and as if I "was there," literally having the experience in real time as it unfolded before me in my mind. Yet it was a memory. Everything I was seeing was in three dimensions exactly like I saw when I was awake.

And in one of those experiences, I remember holding onto an animal before it died. It was some type of rodent — a muskrat or squirrel — or maybe it was a weasel. I held it tightly in my left talon, with its belly facing up towards me. It was still very much alive, looking up at me eye-to-eye, knowing I was going to kill it. We "saw" each other for that moment knowing what the other was going to do. Immediately, I saw its soul leave its body right before I killed it. And then with my right talon, I swiped down at its body and killed it quickly.

What was interesting was that I saw its soul leave its body *before* I killed it. So, I am guessing that the animal felt no pain when my right talon swiped down and killed its biological body. I don't know if that happens in all cases, but my guess is that if I saw it that one time, it probably can happen often with other animals as well.

The other noteworthy experience I had during that eagle lifetime is that I distinctly remember feeling that being an eagle was like being a recluse, a very solo existence that lifetime. It was very familiar, and very comfortable to me, not lonely at all. My mental state was very similar to a previous human monastic lifetime.

In fact, at one point, I recall thinking while I was an eagle, "This is so familiar to me because it reminds me of my previous lifetimes as a monk, and I like that aspect of it." I was recognizing the similarity in solitude, independence and self-sufficiency in both lifestyles.

Chapter 15

Sitting Bull

1831-1890

Playing as a Child

When I was a young boy growing up in Norwood, Massachusetts one of the advantages of our moving into a new house that literally had no landscaping was that we had to plant our own bushes and lawn. And when I say "no landscaping," I mean there was just the house structure surrounded by rock and clay with the bulldozer tracks still left behind, and a driveway connected to a paved street. That was it.

So, my dad had to buy dump truck loads of loam (dirt that was good enough to grow grass and plants in) and I helped him rake and shovel, and eventually, wheelbarrow the loam around the one-acre yard…at least to the extent that a five, six or seven-year old child can "help." It took a few years for us to get the yard planted, doing a section each year.

117

I said moving into this new house was an "advantage" for me anyway, because it meant that, as a 5-year old kid, I always had lots of holes to jump in and hide in, as we planted more bushes and small trees over the years throughout the yard.

I was a kid, right? So of course, I fantasized and used my imagination to make up games.

Consequently, sometimes…okay, often, especially when I was younger…I would take breaks to play while my parents toiled with their shovels, spades, trowels and wheelbarrows. I would help them dig a hole, but I would quickly jump into it making believe I was hiding from the "bad" Indians or from the cowboys who were trying to shoot me…an "Indian." That was the term we used back in the 1950's. We didn't know yet about the terms, "Native," "Indigenous American," etc. I saw myself as an Indian.

I made my own "headdress" consisting of a single feather. Usually in Norwood that meant a crow's feather, or if I was lucky, I would find a beautiful blue jay's feather lying on the ground near my house. Those feathers were small, but I was only five years old, so they fit my small head just fine.

Soon I made my own bow and arrows out of sticks I would find in the woods adjacent to our house. I used some white cotton string from a roll I got from my mom that she used to tie stuff up with. It didn't work very well — the arrows would "fly" about one or two feet, then fall to the ground. But, it was my creation. Somehow I just knew how to make them. I knew the basics anyway. No one had to teach me.

As I got older, I got better at making them and eventually even fastened arrowheads I would shape from rock shavings I would find in the small quarries in the woods near our house where the local construction workers would park their bulldozers as they were building more houses in the development. I fashioned my own quiver out of a cardboard tube to hold my arrows, so I could strap them over my shoulder and reach back easily to grasp and shoot one at a time. Eventually, when I was about eleven years old, I got a fiberglass bow from Ortin's Sporting Goods downtown along with metal tipped arrows, and then I was in business, shooting makeshift targets cut out of cardboard boxes placed in my backyard.

Lenni Lenape Ceremonies

Later in my early teens, I was accepted to be on the staff of the Boy Scout camp in Manomet, Massachusetts — Camp Child. It was located eight miles north of the Cape Cod Canal, near Plymouth. Every other weekend, some of the staff would perform traditional Lenni Lenape ceremonies and dances around a huge campfire on a large sandy beach area next to the half-mile long pond, Morey Hole. I was lucky enough to be one of the dancers.

On Sunday evenings during Visitors Weekend, about 300 campers along with their parents, families and friends gathered around the blazing 10-foot high campfire. The evening always started out with a quiet ceremony imbued with a deep sense of silence and reverence, performed by the four "chiefs," played by four of the older, 18-year old senior staffers. They were in full ceremonial headdress wearing buckskin shirts with decorative bone chest ornamentation, deerskin-fringed pants and moccasins. They each were transported by canoes onto the beach sitting solemnly upright with one brave holding a torch in the bow while the brave in the stern of the canoe silently paddled each of their chiefs to shore from different directions.

It was dramatic, because with no lights anywhere it was so pitch black that if you had never seen the ceremony before, you would be surprised when the braves first lit their torches when the canoes were far offshore about 50-75 yards out in the middle of the pond. Once standing onshore, each of the chiefs passed a peace pipe to the other — raising it to the sky, the earth, and to the four directions. And thus, the festivities of the evening began.

Even though I was a younger staffer, I got to perform in a duet with my tentmate and fellow staffer. It was called the "Challenge" dance. In this dance, both of us wore just a breechcloth and were barefoot. He was barechested, while I wore a bone breastplate. I had one eagle feather in my hair. He only wore a beaded headband.

In this dance, I'm sitting cross-legged on one side of the campfire, while my buddy runs towards me from the opposite side, yelping loudly while he jumps through the huge campfire (he does it fast enough so he never got burned, but I am certain it would never be allowed today). When he lands on my side of the campfire, he buries his tomahawk in the sand at my feet — that is the "challenge." I then pick up the tomahawk and stalk him one revolution around the campfire to the rhythmic beat of our drummers who are sitting off to the side. Then I "kill" him at the end of the dance. And I "toe-heel" dance off quickly and jubilantly to the beat of the drums having defeated my enemy, holding my tomahawk proudly up in the air.

We performed this same dance every other weekend all summer for three summers.

One Sunday night during the two-week period when my Boy Scout troop, Troop 42, happened to be at the camp, we performed that same "Challenge" dance as usual. However, my friend ran a little too fast when he jumped through the blazing campfire and he landed too close to me. So when he swung his arm to bury the tomahawk in the sand, it instead went into my foot. I felt immediate pain, and given that I wore strong prescription eyeglasses back then — of course I had to take them off when I was in the role of a Lenni Lenape warrior — I could not see the damage to my foot. My buddy was also kneeling between the campfire and me, so he was blocking what little light there was. I could only feel my foot with my hand. There was a gash in my right big toe that I estimated was about two inches long. But when I touched my toe and assessed the damage, I also had the thought that I didn't want to scare the 300 people in the audience, especially the little children, so I quickly decided to stoically continue the dance as if nothing had happened.

Of course everyone on staff who was seated right behind me on my side of the campfire saw what had happened. So, when I finished the dance, triumphantly dancing off the sandy beach towards the drummers, the camp nurse was already ready and waiting…as were my parents and siblings who serendipitously were visiting that day.

A half dozen of my fellow staff members immediately lifted my entire body up horizontally over their shoulders and carried me across the sand to the adjacent Administration Building, one of the few buildings in the camp that had electricity. The nurse directed them to lay me down on the ping pong table and put a wooden ruler in my mouth. Some of the guys held down my legs, others held down my shoulders so I wouldn't move suddenly. She then proceeded to take a box of Q-tips and began cleaning out the sand that had gotten caked into my gaping wound. I quickly bit through the ruler, snapping it into three pieces. It was very painful. Nothing was applied to numb the area, she was just trying to clean out as much sand as she could, as fast as she could.

Of course I could hear everyone surrounding me making comments and talking with the nurse as she worked on my foot. I heard someone say it was about two inches long and a quarter of an inch wide. Evidently the wound was so deep that her Q-tips fit all the way down inside this freshly-carved trough in my big toe. One third of my toe had been cut through. She did her best at wrapping it to stop the bleeding sufficiently enough for my parents to drive me to the Emergency Room of the hospital in Plymouth. Two surgeons spent the next two hours using eighteen stitches — nine inside and nine outside — to repair my toe after spending most of their time trying to clean out the rest of the sand first. The surgeons kept asking me, since I was only locally sedated, "What the heck were you doing to get so much sand in this wound?"

They said, "Your pain threshold must be pretty high to have finished that dance like you did." That was the last time I performed the "Challenge" dance at Camp Child.

I also got to perform at this biweekly visitors event in a group "torch tossing" dance involving about a dozen of us, clad only in a loincloth with a rawhide string belt, and no feathers or anything else that might accidentally catch on fire. This was always the finale of the evening performance. I think because of the risks and flaming torches involved, it had a really high "Wow" factor for the audiences.

The drums stopped beating once we had proceeded "toe-heel" to our respective positions encircling the blazing campfire. Then we each leaned in to ignite our torches, and began tossing them in the air, catching them when they came back down. Most of the boys started with just a one revolution flip, followed by a couple of easy revolutions per flip and stayed at that relatively easy level for a while.

Some others of us worked up sooner to tossing the flaming torches higher and higher, each time with more revolutions…until you dropped them in the sand by accident. If you dropped your torch in the sand too many times, then you waited for whomever was still tossing and flipping his torch. I was typically one of the last braves still flipping my torch.

It was difficult because you could not see the wooden "handle" end of the torch while it was airborne — all you could see was the flame. Because it was so pitch black outside when you threw it into the air, the non-burning end disappeared from view almost immediately in the night sky. So you had to develop muscle memory of how hard to toss them and make an educated guess of whether or not you were catching the unlit end. If you misjudged and caught the flaming end, you dropped it immediately to not get burned, but that meant the kerosene-soaked rag nailed to the wooden torch would get sand on it, which would quickly be glowing hot. So the next time you messed up, you would burn your hand on the hot sand on the rag, and drop it immediately. Then you had to wait for the others who were still tossing to finish.

The way you knew how many revolutions you were doing was by practicing during the daytime when you could see both ends of the torch. By developing that muscle memory through practicing over and over, you knew how hard to throw it up in the air to effect a certain number of revolutions.

At night during the ceremonial competition, I could flip it so high and at such a consistent spin rate that three to four revolutions would be my norm. A few times I reached five revolutions. I never got burned.

In retrospect, I think my familiarity with these ceremonies and dance rituals was unusual. I remember feeling a reverence, moved inside very deeply in an unspeakable, inexplicable way whenever the four chiefs were transported onto the shore by their braves in the canoes, followed by their peace pipe ritual. At the time, although I noticed it, I didn't think anything more about that feeling I had.

I was only fourteen to sixteen years old those three summers. Yet I was unusually comfortable with flipping burning torches as high as fifteen to twenty feet in the pitch black air without dropping them when they came back to Earth. And the Challenge dance seemed so "normal" to me, as if I had done similar dances hundreds of times before, with no "foreign" feeling at all. Moreover, I had not thought about my ability to withstand great physical pain until the surgeons pointed it out to me that night in the emergency room.

Thinking back on it now, the power and seriousness with which we teenagers performed these native ceremonies and dances was remarkable. Moreover, it was a testament to how normally and naturally we were taught by our elders to respect the ways of the Lenni Lenape culture we were portraying. Many of us had been elected to the Order of the Arrow, Boy Scouts' National Honor Society which promotes the "habit of helpfulness into a life purpose of leadership in cheerful service to others." The original name for the order *Wimachtendienk, Wingolauchsik, Witahemui* meant "Brotherhood of Cheerful Service" in the native tongue of the Lenni Lenape.

I get emotional even now thinking about what we did back then in the summers of 1965, 1966 and 1967.

Could this have been the beginnings of a recognition memory of a past life, or just a fun summer camp experience of a teenage boy? Who knows. Could it have been both?

The Initial Vision

Since the late 1970's, I've had this recurring memory that has come back over and over again.

At first, it was a vision. I didn't know if it was a past life memory or not. I wondered if I had previously seen this scene in a movie and perhaps was just remembering it from that. So initially I wasn't sure.

The basic vision first came to me like this:

I'm sitting on horseback, as a Native warrior. I cannot see my face, but I can see (and later could feel) my clothes and my horse. I'm on the crest of a hill overlooking a valley below.

Some weeks or months later, more details surfaced. My initial "tunnel vision," which only afforded me a visual of myself, broadened in scope.

Now I could see that I'm on horseback on the edge of a crescent shaped hill overlooking a grassy plain with a river running through it in the distance. I'm in the center position and then on my left side and right side are many braves on horseback. All of them are positioned side-by-side on either side of me — all our faces painted in war paint.

I am wearing a single feather in my hair, and a bone breastplate. We are poised to attack this village of native people down below us at the bend in the river. Everyone is still and quiet, awaiting my command.

To the left and right of me are about thirty braves on each side. We are poised to attack.

That's it. That is the very first vision that I've had vividly etched into my consciousness for four decades since 1979. For many decades that same vision recurred in my awareness from time to time, but with no additional data points, no further "jigsaw puzzle pieces."

Speaking in a Native Language

A strange phenomenon had been happening since the 1980's. I would at times spontaneously begin to speak in what seemed to be a foreign language. I say "seemed to be" because it was gibberish to me, i.e., to my "Kelvin Chin" mind. But another part of me was speaking in what sounded like what were supposed to be "intelligible" languages. At first it seemed like one language, but soon it multiplied to several different-sounding "bodies of speech" that appeared to be linguistically making sense to some part of my subconscious.

I am trying to describe this odd experience in as clear and transparent a way as I can.

I say they seemed like discrete languages because of the way I was stringing the phonetics together. I would pause in the middle for emphasis, and at the ends of "sentences" where it seemed like I was emotionally completing a thought. Again, this was happening without the "Kelvin Chin part of my mind" knowing what the heck my vocal chords were saying . It appeared that I was speaking in several foreign languages (i.e., foreign to me anyway).

It would be in different languages, or seemingly so, since the languages would change and sound different. If I had to guess and label them, I would identify them as Hebrew,

Japanese, Classical Chinese, Native dialects and some languages seemingly so ancient that I didn't recognize them by name at all. Moreover, the feeling I would have would also change to different time periods historically or locations geographically. I could not specify clearly, but sometimes they would "feel" ancient, Middle Eastern, Asian or early North American.

This would spontaneously happen, without any warning, often during my meditations or the rest period afterwards. I have always been in full control when this happens, so I could stop it if I chose to, but in that relaxed state I just let it happen.

And since this started happening in the 1980's, by 2014 this phenomenon was very familiar to me. It became so familiar that the babbling would often happen while I was walking around my apartment on my way to my chair to sit to meditate, as if my psyche "knew" and "experienced" that my energetic system was shifting to a more open state, and so the floodgates would begin opening up even before I sat down and closed my eyes.

For many of those years, I had been "babbling" (it was nonsensical to me, because I did not understand what I was saying) in what sounded like it might have been a Native language. At some point (and I honestly don't know "why" I thought this…), I had the thought that it might be Lakota. And after one of my meditations where this happened (it did not happen in every meditation, it was very random), I wrote down phonetically the sounds I was saying, and did an internet search for what those sounds might mean in words.

To my amazement, I discovered that in that particular meditation I was saying things about going fishing — all in Lakota, a language I had never studied before.

The only movie in which I had ever heard it spoken was in Kevin Costner's award-winning movie, *Dances With Wolves*. As a side note, I found that movie very emotional, but at the time I did not think much of that experience, figuring that many other people probably reacted similarly, since the storyline of the movie had some very emotionally moving content, both in terms of relationships among the characters, as well as the overall Lakota story.

But now, in retrospect, maybe my emotional reaction to that movie might have also been connected to a recognition memory of this past life.

Who Was I?

Since the 1980's, I had had visions in a tipi with other Native leaders, speaking in their native tongue. I was a shaman, at least I was treated as one. I had the "feel" of a shaman. For example, I remembered that I had psychic abilities — I could "hear" voices that spoke to me from invisible beings and I could sometimes foresee future events which played out the way I had seen them in my mind beforehand. So for many years during my 20th century lifetime I assumed I was a shaman in that lifetime in the 1800's.

However, I was confused. Because that memory of being a shaman did not fit in my mind with the initial memory of my leading a large war party all sitting on horseback atop the crescent hill.

Then, in 2014 while I was alone in my living room watching TV in Austin, Texas, I decided to do an experiment. I decided to do an experiment — *on myself*. I thought maybe I could get some deeper insights or information — more "data points," as I often call them — about this lifetime that seemed to have occurred in the 1800's on the Great Plains of America.

Maybe I could figure out who I was.

So, I turned off the TV, went to the internet browser on my laptop and thought I would try to see if I got any "hits" — any unusual experiences when I did a search of some Lakota leaders. For example, I thought maybe I might get some "knowingness" type experience as I had with other past life memories, or maybe I would get an unusual energy surge coursing through my mind and/or body as I had with my initial experience recollecting my crusader life as Richard the Lionheart.

Something. Maybe something like that would happen.

I decided I didn't want to see the names of the Lakota leaders, so I did a search for Lakota chiefs in the 1800's. And I clicked on "Images" so I could only see their faces. Immediately, 100 images (of which twenty to thirty may have been of different Lakota chiefs) appeared on my laptop screen.

Fortunately, the camera was invented in France in 1816, and by 1839 the first cameras landed on the eastern shores of America. So within a few years people were photographing all sorts of people, places and things across the U.S., including the Great Plains natives of America, and in particular the Lakota chiefs.

There were seven different Lakota tribes, each with their own chief. So that naturally resulted in a lot of Lakota chiefs coming and going over the years.

I started clicking through each of the chiefs, again, just looking at their faces to see if I got anything — any recognition of anything.

I clicked on the first one. Nothing.

I clicked on the second one. Nothing.

The third one. Nothing.

I just felt the same. I felt neutral about each of them so far. Nothing special.

It was interesting looking at old black and white photos of native chiefs dressed in their various wardrobes, and posing while sometimes holding certain items (peace pipes, weapons, etc.) obviously specially chosen for that particular moment to be memorialized by this newly invented machine, the camera. This metal box would somehow capture the person's image forever on a piece of paper.

But aside from those thoughts, nothing special was happening "inside" me. And I was conscious of not "trying" to make something happen — I was in a neutral attitude mode. Not expecting anything in particular, but open and receptive to whatever might happen, without knowing what that might be.

So, I continued clicking through the photos.

I got to about the eighth or ninth photo…and then something happened. I had almost given up. In fact, my attitude had just a moment earlier shifted to "Oh, whatever, nice try, Kel…."

And then, all of a sudden, when I clicked on that next photo, I started spontaneously babbling in what I thought sounded like Lakota. I looked at the Lakota chief's face. I did not recognize which one he was.

So, I clicked off of him to the next one. And abruptly, I stopped the spontaneous babbling.

Then I clicked back to the previous one whose photo had me babbling, and I started babbling again…. I still don't know exactly what I am saying, but I am uttering noises that "sound like" Lakota to me. Not that I know what Lakota sounds like exactly — it just "felt like" it was Lakota.

Then I clicked off of his photo. I stopped babbling.

Back on and I resumed babbling. Off, and I stopped.

Back and forth I went, clicking onto and off of that one Lakota chief's photo.

And when I left his photo on my screen, I kept babbling on and on and on.

So, then I looked up his name: Sitting Bull.

I got chills of recognition when I read his name, energy rushes shot through me, similar to what had occurred in me with Richard. Then I researched some facts about Sitting Bull.

And interestingly, it turns out that Sitting Bull was considered a shaman *and* a chief. He was both. Yes, he was the leader of the Hunkpapa Lakota (Sioux), but he was also a holy man, a spiritual leader of his people.

This explained what I had previously thought was a contradiction in my memory of this lifetime. In fact, it was not a contradiction after all.

Also, as I later happened to discover, this would not be the last lifetime where what appeared to be at first a clear contradiction in my memory would subsequently be revealed by historical records to have actually been possible, even highly likely.

Bison in Golden Gate Park

This experience happened when my daughter Sam was a senior at San Francisco State University in 2016. I had flown in from Austin, Texas to see her perform in a dance production at the university. We had gone out to do some errands and had just finished lunch together near the Haight-Ashbury district of San Francisco.

On our way back to her apartment, she said, "Dad, did you know that there are bison in Golden Gate Park?" I said, " No, really?" She said, "Yeah, really there are bison somewhere there in the park. Let's go see if we can find them."

So we drove around inside that big 1000-acre (three-mile by half-a-mile wide) wooded park for a while — there are lots of roads zigzagging this way and that way — and then she recognized and remembered the route to get to where they were. It turns out they're in this very large, 11-acre field in the middle of Golden Gate Park called the Bison Paddock. When we arrived, there were five adult bison in this large meadow, evidently now cared for by staff of the San Francisco Zoo. I later discovered that a herd of bison have been protected there in the park since 1892.

This meadow is the equivalent of more than eight football fields, all fenced in, and wooded on three sides. Since we wanted to get a more unobstructed view of the bison who were off in the distance about 100-200 yards from us, we climbed up onto a bench along the sidewalk, so we could look over the fence.

We both looked at the bison.

And I started crying.

I couldn't help it. Tears just poured out. I couldn't stop crying.

I was just overwhelmed with emotion and sadness. At first I was simply overwhelmed with emotion, no particular thoughts associated with the emotions. Then I had this visceral, palpable feeling like I missed them, those bison. They represented so much to me it seemed. So many emotions were flooding through me — nostalgia, longing, but primarily sadness and grief.

Grief over the loss of many things — the loss of that beautiful animal that had sustained my people and me for so many generations, the loss of that lifestyle I enjoyed so much on the Great Plains, the loss of my family and friends from that lifetime, and more.

I was reconnecting with a lifetime that I'd already, at least superficially, resurfaced for many decades since 1979. But not until this day in Golden Gate Park had I felt so emotionally distraught about that lifetime.

Yes, I had recalled some memories of that lifetime before going to find the bison that day. I knew that I had lived in one of the Plains states in what we now know as the Dakotas as a Lakota shaman and leader of a tribe about 140 years ago. By the time I had this experience in 2016, I had also figured out who I was in that lifetime.

However, I had never been so emotionally moved by my memories as I was at that moment connecting with that herd of bison from the other side of the chain link fence. It caught me by complete surprise. As Sam and I drove away from the meadow heading towards her apartment, I broke down in tears again, and had to pull the car over for a few minutes to calm down and collect myself. Sam held my hand and talked me through it, so that eventually I could continue driving.

As I processed that powerful experience over the subsequent days, I started to resurface visions and memories of the U.S. government, and the white settlers (including I later learned, wealthy New Yorkers who came for the "fun" of it) shooting bison from their trains and wagons. We knew then that the government wanted to kill off bison to "control" us by killing our primary food source. Collectively, they exterminated millions of bison. I remember discussing this fact with our tribal leaders back then, and while we didn't have written proof that it was official government policy, we heard enough stories from soldiers and others for us to easily infer what their not-so-hidden agenda was.

Historians record that "Buffalo Bill" Cody was hired by the Kansas Pacific Railroad to kill bison, killing 4,000 by himself in less than two years — but at least he ostensibly did it to feed railroad workers. Many thousands of other hunters descended on the plains merely for the sport of it.

During a three-year period, 1872-1875, it is estimated that 6,000,000 bison were slaughtered by 10,000 hunters. The bison meat was often left to rot, even though many states outlawed abandoning bison carcasses but never enforced the laws. Yellowstone National Park even forbade the "wanton destruction of fish and game" within the park, but was not staffed to enforce it.

Estimates are that the bison population in North America plummeted from in excess of 60 million in the late 18th century to 541 in 1889. The extermination of the Natives' food supply was highly intentional with the most dramatic decline in bison population between 1840 and 1890. Ironically, that precipitous period of decline overlapped almost perfectly with my lifetime (1831-1890).

Therefore, when I learned that, I thought to myself, "No wonder I had such a strong emotional reaction when I saw a half dozen bison in Golden Gate Park seven years ago." Just over a hundred years earlier, I had literally witnessed firsthand the decimation — the outright slaughter — of tens of millions of bison during my lifetime. I saw the near extinction of the animal that fed, clothed, housed, and provided instruments of protection for my family, friends and loved ones for generations. And, I could do nothing about it.

To underscore how deeply emotionally connected I feel to the bison, the memories that persist in my consciousness the strongest are not the bison hunts we regularly went on, nor the battles we fought with other tribes, and not even the battles we fought with the "blue coats," the soldiers of the U.S. government. It is the starvation we endured after the vast herds of bison were exterminated by or through the tacit support of the U.S. government in order to starve us into submission.

I especially recall the freezing cold winters, in those last years when we escaped to Saskatchewan before we finally gave up and surrendered to the regional government leaders led by those in Washington, DC.

And without a doubt, the most intense emotions I still carry are of the despair and disappointment of having failed to save my people from that terrible end, losing our dignity and our very culture. Those are the memories that linger the deepest in me still today from that lifetime.

Bison Hunt

I had this interesting experience sitting with George Hammond in his living room in 2016 while he and I were meditating together. We decided to do an experiment and see what surfaced. I could "feel" that right below the surface of my awareness was some Native language ready to spontaneously come out. And sure enough, as soon as I closed my eyes, words started pouring out of my mouth in a language I did not know from this lifetime. But interestingly, in this situation I could see visions of what was going on — a bison hunt.

I had visions of being on a bison hunt with a group of my fellow Lakota, galloping on horseback among hundreds maybe thousands of bison racing across a huge open grassy plain. We were all whooping and screaming with excitement, as the physical vibration and deafening sound of the bison thundered all around us.

Then, I saw my close friend fall from his horse about 100 feet away from me. I remembered his name and was calling out to him, while I was sitting next to George. I quickly lost sight of him. He was killed immediately, trampled by the stampeding bison surrounding him. Much later, we found his body.

I was distraught. I cried both in my memory and in George's living room as I recalled my grief over losing my close friend so suddenly and unexpectedly.

George and I discussed the experience after we finished our meditation session together. When I told George what I had seen, he told me that he also had seen a bison hunt when his eyes were closed meditating.

Chapter 16

World War II Fighter Pilot

1918-1943

By the time I was 8-10 years old, I knew most of the World War II fighter and bomber "plane silhouettes" of the U.S. Navy and U.S. Army Air Forces (later known as the U.S. Air Force starting in 1947). While it is true that I did watch war movies as a kid, I did not study planes closely, but somehow seemed to be able to quickly "learn" or maybe even "recognize" which planes were which, even sometimes by simply seeing their silhouettes, their shapes from a distance. Decades before I started recovering my past life memories, I thought it was odd that I had that almost innate capability to recognize planes, including many of the Japanese World War II aircraft (Zeros, Kates, Vals and Bettys), with such ease.

In my childhood or maybe early teens, I remember once watching some World War II movies with actual color footage from the Pacific Theater. In one scene, they were transferring supplies, injured pilots and seamen from ship to ship at sea, suspended in midair using harnesses and chairs attached to cables and pulleys. They were doing this far out in the open ocean — with two huge warships trying to stay as even keeled as possible, but sometimes heaving up and down — I distinctly recall feeling like I had been there, that I had seen it firsthand before in real life.

"In The Mood"

When I was in high school, I played both clarinet and tenor saxophone. I was 2nd chair, 1st clarinet in the concert band, and one of two tenor saxophones in the Stage/Jazz Band.

Without a doubt, the two songs we played, as part of our staple 1969 performance setlist, that I loved the most and that still today move me deeply inside were "Moonlight Serenade" and "In The Mood." Both were 1939 chart-topping hit songs performed by Glenn Miller and His Orchestra, the best-selling recording band in the U.S. from 1939-1942. "In The Mood" was #1 and "Moonlight Serenade" was #3 on the U.S. charts in 1939.

My buddy and I played the clarinet duet in "Moonlight Serenade," and our band ended every concert performance with "In The Mood" — always to a standing ovation from an audience largely made up of parents and relatives whose adolescent and young adult years were during Glenn Miller's prime.

Considering how emotionally moved I was by those two songs, as well as other late 1930's popular "swing era" tunes, makes me wonder if my 1967-1969 high school stage band experience may also have stirred more of those recognition memories. Maybe they were precursors to the memories that started resurfacing in me ten years later in 1978.

Fairfield, Iowa

This memory of my most recent lifetime before incarnating to be Kelvin Chin occurred when I was organizing that Chinese-American TM teacher training program in Fairfield, Iowa in 1978. While I was there, during their summer semester I met a student at that university who would later become my first wife.

At some point during that courtship, I had the "feeling" that I had been a fighter pilot in the Second World War. So in this resurfacing of memories, it first started out as a feeling, not very concrete or tangible at all — no visions, and no strong sense of "knowingness" as I had with some of my other memories. Then over the subsequent weeks, the initially vague feeling became stronger.

Maybe a month or two later, I started having visions of that lifetime — I was blonde, blue-eyed and tall. I lived in San Diego, California where I had done my flight training as a U.S. Navy pilot. I had just gotten married to a beautiful woman there, and we had consummated our marriage days before the Navy shipped me out to the South Pacific in early 1942. I was in my early 20's, the peak years of my sexual maleness.

So, like many other young men in the service, we missed the warmth of our girlfriends and wives. Why else would so many American bombers have long-legged, high-heeled, buxom "dames" prominently painted on the nose of the planes right below the cockpits?

All of those memories flooded into me very quickly and continued over the next several weeks, usually during my meditation program, and sometimes even when I was just out walking across campus or lying down relaxing on the lawns. I even recalled who my wife was in that lifetime…and, yes, who she was then in 1978.

The few intimate moments we had in those memorable days in 1942 — after our marriage ceremony, before I left San Diego and the United States for the last time in that lifetime — had yielded no offspring. She and I had married very young, as was the norm in that generation, especially during wartime.

I have often wondered if the reason I continue to be emotionally attracted to popular women's fashion styles and body types of the 1940's is because I died so young that time, and missed out on those years as a young man at the peak of his virility, with a gorgeous wife with whom to grow a wonderful family. Essentially, *vita interrupta* ("a life interrupted"). Instead, I was cast into the cauldron, into "do or die" situations in my 20's...only to die shortly thereafter.

F4F Wildcats

Within the next few years, more details would pop into my mind, in a piecemeal fashion — a little more of this part and then that part of that life. Much like the creation of a jigsaw puzzle.

Later in the 1980's and 1990's, I began remembering flying my Grumman F4F Wildcat fighter plane off of aircraft carriers. I don't know how I knew the type of plane. I just knew. First, we did training takeoffs and landings on marked and measured field runways in San Diego, later off of flattops offshore, and eventually in the South Pacific on the open seas. Then, I remembered the name of my carrier — the USS Enterprise.

I recalled the feeling of being very focused, setting aside any fear, as I landed my plane sometimes on a carrier deck that was pitching and rolling, and having to compensate in split second movements of my stick, pedals and throttle to adjust for the ship's movements in order to successfully land my plane on the deck, my tail hook grabbing the arresting cable.

I had many memories of both fighting Japanese fighters and bombers, as well as strafing and bombing runs on ground targets located on jungle islands in the Pacific. I sometimes wonder if my habit of routinely checking all my mirrors in a split second while driving my car now on a highway is related to those times when developing that habit of "checking your twelve o'clock, three o'clock, your nine o'clock and your six" was a necessity, and could mean the difference between life or death, being the shooter or getting shot down.

Early on in the resurfacing of my memories, sometime in the 1980's, I had a very clear memory of being shot down and being engulfed in flames while trapped in my cockpit as my plane plummeted out of the skies over the South Pacific in early 1943. I was about twenty-five years old.

F4F Wildcat, carrier-based World War II fighter

That is another lifetime where I remember how I died. It was not a pleasant way to go. While my mind left my body before I could feel the physical pain, it was still very painful emotionally watching my body burn, unable to slide open the jammed canopy and eject from my cockpit.

A Field in San Francisco

One evening in 2015, when I was visiting my daughter Sam at SFSU, she and I drove to pick up her boyfriend after work. He worked as a swim instructor at an indoor pool facility called La Petite Baleen Swim Schools which is located on Mason Street near the base of the Golden Gate Bridge in San Francisco.

We parked our car in their parking lot, and while we waited for him to finish, I got out and walked by myself towards the bay to an open, grassy, very flat field. The field was between Mason Street and the bay. Mason was the road we had driven in on, which is below Route 101 (the road that goes over the Golden Gate Bridge).

Normally I would have stayed in the car and chatted with my daughter whom I hadn't seen in months. What drew me to walk that 150 feet out into the middle of that field? I don't know. In retrospect, it's puzzling at best. Maybe I just wanted some space since I had just flown in from my home in Austin, Texas to see one of my daughter's many dance performances — I never missed any of them — and traveling is always a bit hectic. So, a quiet moment by myself on a beautiful night in San Francisco before I got back in the car with my daughter and her boyfriend made sense.

Anyway, I walked out to the middle of the huge field, just to feel the very settled vibe, and breathe the peaceful fresh air under the moonlit sky. It was a beautiful evening.

The pool parking lot was at a dead end road. So there were no other cars or traffic within eyesight or earshot of us. All the kids and their parents had long ago left the pool at closing time, 8:00 PM. It was around 9:00 PM by now.

This was one of those unusual moments that you don't foresee happening…

Then it happened.

There was an unmistakable feeling. Something oddly settling.

I stood still. Letting myself experience it. Whatever "it" was. I didn't know what it was. I had no inkling as to why or what had happened…some vague, nondescript feeling. I just stood there for another minute or two.

Then I walked back through the moist-with-evening-dew, almost manicured-cut grassy field to the parking lot and our rental car. By then, my daughter's boyfriend had turned off the lights and locked the doors at the pool, and was standing with her outside the car.

I didn't immediately tell them of my experience.

My first comment to him after I said the usual greetings was, "What's up with that big huge field there? How come some developer hasn't put up a bunch of condos overlooking the bay and the Golden Gate Bridge and made a killing? It seems like a perfect place for it. On a dead end street like this? Quiet, a gorgeous view?"

He said, "Oh, that's a park now. It used to be an airfield years ago."

Whoa.

So, I told the kids I'd be right back, that I wanted to go out there again on the field for a minute. That's all I said.

I walked back out to the middle of the field and looked it over from a different perspective. It was really dark and it was only lit by the moon, but it was bright enough so that I could see pretty far down in front of me — far enough to imagine that, yes, this is a long enough field to have been an airfield for early propeller planes. I must have been standing on what used to be a cement runway, but was now a nicely-mowed grassy field.

And then I got a rush of energy. I suddenly felt very emotional. Then I could "see" planes flying in and out of the field, and I remembered I had flown in and out of this very field when I was a very young man in a previous lifetime. Since I have never been a pilot in my current 20th century lifetime, and planes weren't invented until 1903, it must have been my immediate previous lifetime in the 1920's, 30's and 40's.

Later that evening I researched online about that field and discovered it had been a military airfield. It was called Crissy Airfield. According to the National Park Service website: "From 1921 to 1936 Crissy Army Airfield was the center of West Coast military aviation. During these years of explosive advances in air power, pilots from Crissy performed maneuvers and mock battles, flew endurance flights, surveyed the west by air, and scouted for forest fires."

However, the records tell us that after the construction of the Golden Gate Bridge was completed in 1933, the flight patterns were so hampered by the bridge that regular flights out of the airfield were curtailed and then eventually stopped a few years later around 1936. The very last flights out occurred in 1974.

Well, that explained a lot.

I learned that the grassy field was well maintained now by the National Park Service since 1994, replacing what was a cement field of runways. Since it was so dark when we were there, I could not see any of the still existing original military buildings along the edge and up the hillside from the field. But that's why it was so incredibly flat, which I had thought seemed odd for land immediately next to a huge body of water, the San Francisco Bay. My research revealed that in the 1800's, and earlier, the area had in fact been a marshy swamp — which made a lot more sense to me — before it was converted by the military.

So, was that another recognition memory? Perhaps. I'm not sure how else to explain the unusual emotional response I had from merely standing in an open field that I didn't yet know had been an airfield, never mind a military airfield.

Conflicting Memories?

I have two very distinct memories from this World War II lifetime: flying off of aircraft carriers and hiding from Japanese soldiers in the jungle. These two seemingly conflicting memories have co-existed in my mind since the late 1970's.

Since I never thought I'd be discussing these past life memories, I just let that conflict sit in my mind without much further thought, other than, "Hmmmm...that doesn't make sense, but oh well...." After all, what would a fighter pilot who's flying off aircraft carriers be doing hiding from Japanese soldiers in a hot, muggy jungle? I suppose I could have been shot down and gotten stuck on some jungle island in the South Pacific. That was a possible logical explanation. So I left it at that.

The aircraft carrier landings and other "at sea" memories were very clear as I said. However, the jungle memories were equally clear — I could even hear the Japanese in the jungle approaching our little pup tents...that's how close the enemy soldiers were to our encampments. I remember being petrified with only a sidearm pistol to protect myself against potentially many dozens of much better armed, "fight until you die" battle-hardened Japanese infantrymen.

I recall crawling on my belly in the underbrush and mud, trying to get away. And I can still hear the crackling sound of a walkie talkie as it goes dead when the U.S. soldier on the other end is killed and all you hear are the sounds of Japanese soldiers speaking in Japanese and the noise of their progress through the jungle brush.

Then more recently in about 2018, I stumbled across a documentary about the war in the Pacific in 1942-43 after the attack on Pearl Harbor which occurred on December 7, 1941. I learned that in the Battle of the Eastern Solomons in which the Japanese attempted to retake the crucial airfield on Guadalcanal, on August 24, 1942 the aircraft carrier USS Enterprise had been badly damaged by "Val" dive bombers. The number 2 (midship) and number 3 (aft) elevators — two of the three elevators that bring planes below decks for repair, refueling and rearming, and then bring them back up for take-offs — were incapacitated. As a result, many of the Enterprise aircraft were unable to land back on their carrier. Some instead landed at Henderson Field on the island of Guadalcanal. A number of those pilots stayed on Guadalcanal in the defense of the island, adding their planes to the already existing force stationed there specifically to protect that strategically critical airfield. In addition to attacks from air and sea, there were also many accounts of the Japanese infantry trying to retake Henderson Field, attacking frequently from their jungle positions on the island.

So, that could also be a credible explanation for my memories of flying off aircraft carriers, along with memories of hiding from attacking Japanese in a hot, humid jungle environment. I have very clear memories of intense, humid heat (perhaps of Guadalcanal?), and then taking off with my canopy open, climbing and feeling the air get cooler and cooler, until…ecstasy. One could breathe freely again without feeling stifled.

I read that in describing what it was like to stand near Henderson Field in the heat and humidity of Guadalcanal, Major Marion Carl, a fighter ace, described it as "…the only place on Earth you could stand up to your knees in mud and still get dust in your eyes." He was part of what was called the "Cactus Air Force," a motley collection of pilots and planes from the U.S. Navy, Marines and Army Air Forces who protected Henderson Field from the almost daily Japanese air, sea and land attacks. "Cactus" was the U.S. military code name for the island of Guadalcanal.

Maybe I found myself on Guadalcanal for a while fighting as part of the Cactus Air Force before I could rejoin my carrier crew mates. That could have been a possible explanation for those two, initially at least, seemingly conflicting memories.

Swimming in Hawthorne, California

On January 9, 2023, while swimming laps in the city pool, as I regularly have done three times a week for the past several years, I had an unusual experience. When I've exercised regularly over the years doing repetitive physical motions, like jogging, rowing, long-distance cycling or lap swimming, I've recognized that familiar feeling I sometimes get where my body is performing the physical motions of the exercise, but my mind can become disengaged and almost "off in its own world."

Over the years, when this has happened, I usually just "space out" without having anything noteworthy drift through my mind. This time, however, was different.

I was on my 8th or 9th lap of backstrokes, when I found myself getting flash memories of a period around 1917-1918, long before I was born this lifetime as Kelvin Chin. I saw myself on the Other Side observing what was going on "down here" on Earth at that time — World War I was well into its third year.

While in the pool, I got the distinct impression that something from my past as a former military leader had informed me in 1917 or 1918 of potential world events that might transpire much later. When I was swimming getting these insights and intuitions, while I wasn't sure what they were precisely from historically, I somehow knew that my lifetimes as a military and political leader of nations played a part in my decision to incarnate again. I think those prior experiences had given me an ability to see the more long-range effects of certain treaty agreements, and especially the undesirable concessions that were often involved, usually out of necessity.

In particular, for no apparent reason at that point, my lifetime as Frederick of Prussia swept through my mind as relevant to this experience somehow. When that happened, I even chuckled out loud while I was swimming, and shouted, "That was weird!" Since I was only one of four people in the big city pool on that rainy day, I'm sure no one heard me.

That was my experience in the swimming pool. I did not know what events may have precipitated my relative certainty that dire consequences would probably result after the 1918 end to the First World War.

So, when I finished swimming, I researched when that war ended and when the Treaty of Versailles was signed. It turns out that it ended on November 11, 1918 (which is why Veterans Day in the U.S. is always on November 11th), and the Treaty was signed on June 28, 1919.

However, my sense was that whatever had been resurfacing in my mind when I was in the pool had occurred before 1919. So I researched some of the events that led up to the end of the war and before the treaty was signed.

Here is what I discovered.

I think the "tipping point" for me to decide to incarnate again may have been the surrender of Russia to Germany in early 1918. Evidently, the treaty that was finalized was devastating to Russia. The humiliating terms of the treaty effectively surrendered one third of Russia's population, half of her industry and 90% of her coal mines to Germany. Russia also gave up large swaths of land, including Poland, Ukraine and Finland, as well as significant cash payments to Germany to release Russian prisoners.

I did not know those details until after I swam. But remember as I mentioned, when I was swimming, I had gotten the distinct impression that my prior lifetimes as a military leader of countries, most notably of Prussia, was somehow connected to my incarnating sooner than later.

Perhaps while I was on the Other Side, equipped with my knowledge of having previously fought against and negotiated with the Russian political and military leaders in the 1700's, I surmised that their mindset would not be very fond of the terms of their agreement with Germany in 1918. That their generations-old contempt for the Germans would not only be harbored but expressed in a future conflict. And I guessed that it could very well be those "sore wounds," that might be the source down the road, of inflaming a future military conflict between the nations. Maybe it was that treaty that I saw as untenable, that would be a source of imbalance and shame…even though it impacted Russia, not Germany, in a negative way.

Maybe that was enough of a red flag to me that this war — World War I — was not going to be "the war to end all wars"....

In retrospect, I wonder if the leadership in Russia almost wanted to "bait" Germany into the Second World War when they conspired with Germany to circumvent the Versailles Treaty terms that explicitly disallowed Germany from engaging in any arms development or production. To get around that clear prohibition, the Russians invited the German scientists and munitions experts to secretly build and test new tanks and other military technology instead on Russian soil from 1920-26. Perhaps key Russian leaders knew all along they would steal the new German technology and execute all the scientists involved, once they had the military secrets, which is exactly what they did.

I think I may have "seen" that likelihood from the Other Side, and maybe that prompted me to come back, born in late 1918 or 1919. Who knows — my assessment of the Russian feelings about their treaty with Germany are conjecture. But they do fit with the distinct experience I had in the pool — that my lifetime as Frederick of Prussia somehow informed my decision to incarnate in order to participate in what would later manifest as, when I was in my 20's, the Second World War.

Two Random Reconnections?

In 2015, I helped a friend die. There was a team of us actually. One day a few weeks before he died, I went to the hall bathroom in their house in Round Rock, Texas. As I had many times before, I glanced down at their round throw rug and the abstract pattern of different shapes surrounded by many hundreds of small dots. Most people would probably "see" those dots as stars. However, this time something about them jumped out at me. And what I saw were hundreds of planes flying in formation — all those little starry-looking dots reminded me of planes. In particular, those dots triggered the vision in my mind of hundreds of F4F Wildcat fighter planes over the Pacific Ocean. And flying next to me in that vision from the early 1940's was my friend, who was now dying down the hallway in his bedroom.

Another reconnection happened in 2019 when I was invited to speak at a conference on the East Coast. I met and connected deeply with a former U.S. Air Force pilot who served in the Vietnam War. He and I had the strong sense, call it a "knowing," that he had been my wingman in the 1940's when we flew F4F Wildcats, and that he continued on to fly Corsairs after I was killed in action.

In these two examples, I was struck by how randomly these "bread crumbs," that may inform us about our past lives, can surface. Sometimes seemingly out of nowhere, and often in the most unlikely of situations.

In the first example, my memory was stimulated by an abstract image on an inanimate object, a rug. And in the second example, my memory was stirred up by a chance face-to-face meeting with someone I had never met before in this lifetime.

So that lifetime during the Second World War as an F4F U.S. Navy fighter pilot was my most recent lifetime before my current one. I was on the Other Side for about eight years before deciding to come back.

Chapter 17

From Non-Belief To Rational Acceptance

Before I continue with more of my stories, here is a little background on my formative years this lifetime and where my beliefs started out from, including how I much later started to piece together "threads" from these different lifetimes that seemed to "tie them together." At first, however, I didn't even believe in an afterlife, never mind consider something as bizarre sounding as reincarnation.

My Family Background and Original Belief

In 1977, when my first past life memories started resurfacing, I did not believe in reincarnation. I went to church when I was a kid growing up in Norwood, but I didn't believe in heaven. I thought when we died, that was it. We got buried and our one "life" had ended.

I was raised in a science-based family. My dad graduated from Northeastern University as a mechanical engineer and my mom earned her degree in chemistry from Boston University.

My mom named me after Lord William Thompson Kelvin. He is the British mathematician, mathematical physicist, and engineer who did important work in the formulation of the First and Second Laws of Thermodynamics, and for whom absolute temperatures are stated in units of "kelvin" in his honor. While the existence of a coldest possible temperature (absolute zero) was known prior to his work, Lord Kelvin is known for determining its correct value as approximately −273.15 degrees Celsius or −459.67 degrees Fahrenheit.

So I was steeped in math and science both from my parental upbringing, as well as from my own focus on those two subject areas when I was growing up. Therefore, I knew from an early age that math and science were areas that aspired to develop a "right" and "wrong" view — an absolute view — of the universe.

Consequently, my lack of belief in reincarnation was not merely superficial. It was deep in my core. It did not fit with my view from a math and science standpoint. How could you prove it, like you could the theorems I studied in high school geometry? You couldn't.

So, when I heard others talking about past lives, I immediately dismissed it as "crazy talk" based on very colorful imaginations. My belief was just like my dad's, "When we die, we go in a box, they throw the dirt on us, and we're done!" — my dad's famous line he repeated freely, whether asked or not. My mom was by comparison silent on the subject. She was less vocal with her views but leaned heavily in this direction as well.

But, as you can imagine, when I started having these highly unusual experiences that I have shared with you, my "math and science" mind could not process them. So, at first I rejected the experiences as figments of my imagination.

However, fortunately I had learned to meditate about seven years before these "weird" experiences started happening. And even though my objective for learning to meditate was to reduce my anxiety which had skyrocketed at the beginning of my sophomore year at Dartmouth, meditation had some unintended positive side effects.

I started feeling more connected inside with myself, which manifested at first in my feeling less stressed, and more stable and secure. Soon thereafter, I started to feel a lasting inner peace and feeling of expansion from within that spilled over to when I was awake walking around campus and going to classes. Then I began to have feelings of deep connection with my surroundings, both animate and inanimate — a very difficult feeling to describe or explain with my then "math and science" mind. Nevertheless it was a real experience. And it was not explainable in mathematical or scientific terms.

So I was lucky to have that as a backdrop prior to my influx of experiences in 1977. As I began to have that flood of seeming past life memories washing through my consciousness over the subsequent decades, I somewhere stumbled across the idea of the First Law of Thermodynamics — that "energy cannot be created nor destroyed." That led me to wonder if that could possibly be an explanation for why my mind seemed to continue after my biological bodies had died over multiple lifetimes over and over. So that is what I have pinned it to all these years, because out of everything I have heard or read about, that seems to make the most sense to my "math and science" mind — my logical, rational mind.

Speaking of math and science, let's get one thing out in the open and on the table. I don't think there is any "proof" that any of these experiences are "absolutely" accurate memories of our past lives.

I don't think that is possible because, as I said, the scientist in me tells me that "proof" means there is a right or wrong answer. It is black or white. There is no in-between answer. That's what proof means. It is how a true scientist defines "proof."

By contrast, when I reflected on my experiences, there was no such "absoluteness" of proof. I had only my *interpretations* of those experiences.

Now, could I possibly assess those interpretations to see how *more or less* accurate they might be? Yes, of course. However, realizing that it was impossible and therefore pointless, I gave up trying to find a way to *absolutely* prove that my assessment was "ironclad" accurate.

So what did I start to look at to get a better sense if my past life experiences were real or imaginary?

As I have continued to assess those experiences through my own inherent filter of "born-with-it skepticism," the following are some of my "ah-ha" moments that have helped me start to figure out what was going on within myself during these past 45 years. I will lay them out one by one, but I am only doing so for clarity purposes — not to imply that there is some step-by-step process I've gone through every time.

Since the jigsaw puzzle pieces come very randomly and they never have the very useful box cover picture for guidance, I've found that any help I can get in piecing the disparate pieces together is helpful. These several ideas have been instrumental in assisting me in "piecing together these many different jigsaw puzzles."

The Emotional Element

The first thing I've tended to notice is my emotional feeling from the past life memories. I've noticed that most of my initial memories of a given past life have been from very strong emotional experiences. I think the more intense it is, the more likely it is connected to something real.

Why? Because our emotions tend to be our "default" internal drivers. They tend to be the precursors to our conscious thoughts, i.e., what happens automatically deep inside us before we even think. My very first experience with my Simon Peter lifetime, for example, was from a very intense, emotional dream.

The Sensory Element

I also look at how sensory the experience is. The more powerful the sensory experience, the more likely it is a resurfacing of a memory of something that really happened. In addition, the more senses that are involved — sight, touch, taste, smell, hearing — the more probable the memory is real.

For example, the physical sensation of being roasted in the searing heat under a cloudless sky while floating on the Mediterranean Sea when I was the shipwrecked Carthaginian slave, or the feel of my shoulder, chest and back muscles as I swung my broadsword in battle breathing through dust-filled nostrils on the battlefields of the Middle East as Richard the Lionheart.

The Third-Party Element

I've found that another reliable factor to look for is information that is "third-party" based. Third-party means information that existed and others knew it, but that I did not know before having the experience. There could be multiple different types of such sources.

For example, this could be information that I, as Kelvin Chin, did not previously know. But that is available in existing books, documents, letters, journals written by people I have never studied or met. Or perhaps, yelling the word "Saracens" without knowing what it meant, or recognizing a photo of a Lakota chief on the internet whom I had never seen before in this lifetime.

It could be types of ships, languages, or word usage in a certain context only used in that earlier time period. For example, the multilevel ships powered by slave oarsmen and the boarding device call the *corvus* designed by the Romans used against the Carthaginians in only one of the three Punic Wars, or speaking Japanese while wielding a samurai sword.

Or, it could be people living in the 20th or 21st century whom I had never met, but who may "recognize or identify" me from a past life relationship. Take for example, the story as told to me in 2020 by William Baldridge of Charlie Lutes referencing in 1973 the existence of both Simon Peter and Frederick the Great as being the same TM teacher in Maharishi Mahesh Yogi's organization, yet Lutes was lecturing about this to people I had never met, several years before I had any past life recollections.

Those are some of the various filters I've come up with to look through in order to better assess whether a given experience I've had may actually have been from a previous lifetime. Again, it is not foolproof, but it is a way to assess the experience with more reliable evidence when it's available.

But, at the end of the day, is it that important to me to be even "pretty sure" my experiences are valid past life memories? No.

Not at all.

Why? Because I am defined by my present, what I am choosing to do now. Not what I may or may not have chosen to do in the past.

Can I learn from what may seem to be past life memories?

Absolutely yes. And that's how I choose to view them. That is the important question I ask myself in each instance.

"Know Thyself"

For me, the primary reason for paying attention to information I may get from resurfacing past life memories is to help me learn more about myself:

"Know thyself"

That is how I view my own self-development — gaining greater self-knowledge, applying it, seeing what works and what doesn't, in a given life situation. To me, that's useful learning.

I've never merely stopped at the Who, What, When and Where. Instead, I've always "turned within" and looked more inside.

What about that past life memory tells me more about Kelvin Chin…about what makes *me* tick?

Why do I sometimes have a knee-jerk reaction to like certain things in life, and have equally spontaneous dislikes for other things — things that give me pleasure versus things that I may find unpleasant?

I've found in my journey that knowing where that comes from in my past has helped me "unlock" certain self-knowledge that has proven helpful in accentuating my desire for and improving my ability to find certain likable things in my life, and diminishing the negative effects of unlikable things. In short, it has helped me make better choices, especially ones that are more aligned with my desires.

For me, my past life memories have been one of many sources of self-knowledge. Since the maxim "Know thyself" sums up the objective of my journey through life, I have paid attention to these memories and contemplated them in this pragmatic way, using them to inform me better about how to live more effectively with greater fulfillment — as Kelvin Chin. In this way, these memories have enhanced my level of contentment and inner peace this lifetime, in my continual present.

Chapter 18

Personality Traits
Traversing the Millennia

What *continues* after we die?

Of course we can say, generally speaking, that our mind (or soul, spirit, consciousness) continues after our biological body dies. But is there something more specific that we can study and learn from that is unique to each of us and seems to continue from lifetime to lifetime?

I think so. I call it our "personality."

Following are some personality traits of several of the figures I have previously described in this book. I will attempt to give as much background detail as possible in sharing my own memories illustrative of various traits, accompanied with historically known real life examples of the respective personality traits of the individual being discussed. For that reason, I will be discussing only those lifetimes where the person has historically known character traits that have been researched by third parties — professional biographers and historians.

Chapter 19

Personality

Simon Peter

1 B.C.-67 A.D.

Stubborn

Simon who was later called Simon Peter, most commonly known historically simply as "Peter," lived about 2,000 years ago. Jesus called him "Peter" because that is the translation for the Greek word "rock."

I think the reason Jesus called Simon "the rock" was because it reflected what Jesus immediately saw that characterized Simon's personality when they first met: stubbornness. One might more politely say "initially immoveable," or hard to convince.

I was the opposite of gullible.

I remember there were many hundreds of so-called "messiah-wanna-be's" preaching throughout Judea and the surrounding regions at the time. I was largely skeptical of all of them. I had to be convinced that any of them were worth my time away from my fishing business. After all, we had to catch fish to sell, make money to buy food to support my wife, daughter...and mother-in-law with whom my brother Andrew and my family lived. Spirituality was great, but we needed to also be practical — that was my thinking.

So, when my brother Andrew suggested that I go with him to hear some "great, wise teacher" — or some such phrase he used to persuade me to go see John the Baptist — I was initially reluctant. But I went because my brother was not known to be a flaky guy. If anything, he was the opposite. He thought things through, almost to a fault. Meaning that he was always thinking about things. And then, thinking about what he thought about thinking about those things. "Lighten up!" I would often teasingly tell Andrew.

But he was a good brother, and trustworthy. Reliable. Not easy traits to find in anyone, never mind your own brother.

When John (the Baptist) met Jesus, I remember that while I was excited, I was still skeptical. This guy Jesus had to prove himself to me. I could not merely rely on my brother's opinion, or John's. I had to make up my own mind.

Emotionally Inspired Leadership

When Jesus asked me to be the spokesperson for his group of teachers, known as apostles (a Greek word that simply means "one who is sent out" to teach), I was not nervous. I knew I could do whatever was asked of me. I was confident.

That, however, does not mean I didn't recognize my need to further understand his teachings. Consequently, I took all opportunities to ask him questions, sometimes repeatedly, until

I understood what he meant. Sometimes this would be to the humorous chagrin of my brother who typically understood ideas, even new ideas, the first time around. I was a slower learner than Andrew.

I actually have recollections of sometimes maybe even being (seen as) annoying, though not intentionally, by how many questions I had. Why did I ask so many questions?

Because I had an emotional need to understand what he was saying.

And I was secure within myself to ask. I wasn't embarrassed. When you have that emotional need to understand — all other emotions be damned! Understanding trumps everything else.

I felt that the better I understood it — even the simplest of his messages, for example, about "love" as acceptance — the more effective I would be at teaching it to others. To me, that deeper understanding, not merely a superficial one, was the key to being able to inspire others.

I learned this from my own personal experience of gaining inspiration from having understood new ideas myself when they were first placed before me. That moment of understanding when the epiphany happens is the fundamental basis of what I call "emotionally inspired leadership and teaching."

But the understanding must precede the leadership, at least for me. The leadership is founded on the understanding. And the understanding is the basis of the emotional reaction. Not vice versa. Without a proper understanding of the idea, the emotion is baseless, empty, fleeting, easily replaced by another emotion when the energy of the original one subsides. I realized that's why mere memorization and recitation of his teachings, without a full understanding of them, were so much less impactful. Again, that's how I am wired. Others may work it in reverse order. But I learned that about myself long before I met up with Jesus again in Judea that lifetime.

In going through that process with Jesus so many times in Judea, I learned from him how to duplicate that learning process. I learned how to lead others in a more powerful and effective way. He taught me how important understanding was in order to build a genuine, self-generated emotional force within one's messages. Because then that emotion was coming from my own self-revelation. That emotion and enthusiasm found its source in my personal excitement — the thrill derived from that deeper understanding. That is what I could then impart to my students — both the enthusiasm *and* the content. And that made my teaching and lecturing so much more effective than merely attempting to transfer a feeling to my students, like I had seen so many other teachers focus on doing.

I also remember seeing him demonstrate to us — without saying he was, he just did — how to be loving and acceptant of others and what that did to the human dynamic between the individual and him. It opened them up, they felt secure to be themselves, and I watched him "see" into them, who they really were deep inside. In the same way, I had personally experienced him doing that with me, and those around me who spent so much time with him.

I aspired to emulate that skill that he innately owned. In making continued attempts at refining that skill through practicing it as often and with as many as I could, I added another dimension to my emotionally inspired leadership and teaching lifeskill. I continue to refine and hone that skill today.

Public Speaker

Peter was known for his ability to speak to small and large audiences, grab their attention, and get Jesus's teachings across in a digestible form. It was Jesus's teaching me how to teach and how to share knowledge that made my work so much more effective than it otherwise would have been.

I had learned how to touch others with my words, how to touch them deeply inside. Interestingly, it was a skill I have had to manage at times, because I discovered at a young age that my words could also be cutting and hurtful. Meting that out in an appropriate way at the appropriate time is something I have learned over the millennia, and am still refining.

While I remember having had a great deal of opportunity to practice public speaking when I was an Egyptian priest thousands of years earlier, under Jesus's tutelage I honed it even further.

Passionate Impetuousness and Pragmatism

While Peter was never a military leader in that lifetime, he did know how to wield a knife. There is that story of him with one swipe, cutting off the ear of the soldier who came to the olive garden to arrest Jesus, where Peter acted rashly responding to his strong internal emotional reaction.

Even though none of us were surprised that Jesus was eventually arrested, it was still a shock to all of us when it actually happened. Well, at least my brother Andrew and I weren't surprised. I can't speak for the other apostles. But I remember speaking almost constantly with my brother, day and night for several days before Jesus was arrested, about what he thought would happen to our teacher…and when.

Andrew and I were very open with each other. I was more close-lipped with the others as I did not want to scare them by sharing with them what my brother and I saw unfolding before our eyes.

It took my brother a while to convince me that the miracles that Jesus was performing were a mistake. It was clear that Jesus was getting increasingly frustrated with the masses. He had initially been attracting groups of maybe 50, 100, a couple hundred or more, but very few were practicing what he was teaching. Moreover, the size of the crowds started dwindling, some very small groups even of just three or four showing up for a class out on a street corner or a field.

So, in his frustration, maybe he thought if he got bigger crowds, more would listen and hear. That's when the miracles became not just a sporadic thing, but became a regular part of his daily routine. Eventually even many times a day. This attracted huge crowds of course. But it was made up of just sightseers, people there for the circus act, for the show. Not true "seekers" of self-realization. Not the ones who really wanted to practice "knowing thyself."

And that frustrated Jesus even more. So his frustration grew to anger. Not just the occasional anger and frustration we all would express, including him, around the campfires at night, but an undercurrent of frustration and anger that, quite frankly, scared me. It scared me because I was afraid of what might happen to him.

I think he knew what was going to happen that night in the grove, and why with such fervor that night he told all of us, "Protect yourselves. Whatever happens, you need to continue the teaching." After all, he had called out our fellow apostle Judas Iscariot at dinner earlier that same evening. Why else would he do that and then instruct us shortly afterwards to protect ourselves at all costs? In retrospect, it seems obvious. I think he knew exactly what they would do to him.

And so, being the pragmatist that I am, in order to fulfill the instructions of my teacher to "do whatever it takes to continue the teaching," when I was later asked if I knew him, I said, "No way…" — unwittingly fulfilling his prophecy.

Saying otherwise would have gotten me arrested along with him, and probably killed as well. I was conflicted, no doubt… which is why Andrew found me the next morning crying all night in a ditch along the side of the road. And why he could not console me or convince me to quickly go see my teacher one more time before he expired on the cross and transitioned from his dead biological body.

Mediator and Meditator

I remember having an interest-based negotiation style when I was Richard, but my brother Andrew who is now George Hammond reminded me that he and I engaged in similar "mediative" tactics with Jesus.

After John the Baptist was killed, Jesus traveled to meet with the leaders of John's group. Jesus was accompanied by Peter, his brother Andrew, John the apostle, and several others. In meeting with John the Baptist's followers soon after his death, we all hoped to accomplish two things: first, of course to offer condolences and solace to them, and second, to attempt to have them join our group under Jesus's leadership to help us continue teaching what John had started, since this was a joint project to be led by both John and Jesus. Andrew and I had previously been students of John's before he instructed us to go with Jesus a few years earlier, so we had a special place in our hearts for John and his work. However, while a few of his followers joined us in our teaching work, most didn't.

At that meeting, Jesus also attempted to teach them how to meditate. He said, "Just close your eyes and seek the Kingdom of Heaven within." Again, we met with limited success in teaching them how to meditate, but by then it had become easy and effortless for us since we had already sat with Jesus in that meditative state so often.

Chapter 20

Personality

Marcus Aurelius

121-180 A.D.

Marcus Aurelius is primarily known for being a philosopher and student of the ancient Greek school of Stoicism. He is also considered one of the "Five Good Emperors" of the Roman Empire (a term coined 1,300 years later by Niccolò Machiavelli). In addition, he was the last emperor of the *Pax Romana*, an age of relative peace, calmness and stability for the Roman Empire lasting from 27 B.C. to 180 A.D.

Early Study of Philosophy

Marcus Aurelius's interest in philosophy was already deeply engrained in his psyche very early in his life. I remember studying in my early childhood in ancient Rome as a member of the wealthier class of Roman citizens, the patricians. When

I started having these memories, I didn't know who I was, but I was fascinated and driven by the study of philosophy — how to think in a way that helped me make sense of my thoughts and emotions, and how to navigate the world. That's how I viewed what others called "philosophy." I viewed it as how to live life by applying my knowledge of how I fit into the universe.

To me, philosophy is completely practical. To not think philosophically — in the way I defined it above — seemed impractical to me then, and still does now.

Historians also record that Marcus was so devoted to the study and practice of being a philosopher that when he was a young boy, it took a great deal of cajoling and deft persuasion by his mother to get him to wear clothes befitting a young man being groomed by the emperor Hadrian to be his successor. Instead, Marcus chose to wear the plain coarse-fibered garb preferred by philosophers.

In addition, Marcus was so taken with "living the life of a philosopher" that his mother had a difficult time convincing the stubborn child to stop sleeping on the floor at night, as was the habit of a 2nd century philosopher. Finally, after much coaxing, she got the young boy to sleep in his bed.

Humility

I recall having a deep dislike of pomp. It struck me as an unnecessary show of arrogance and narcissism. It still does.

Marcus only appeared at formal ceremonies and received honorific titles as was the cultural norm in Rome because he had to. He knew it was considered part of his role as emperor, so he perfunctorily performed those ceremonial duties out of respect for his culture and his position within it. Marcus never lost his desire to be a "regular person" preferring to (although he couldn't) happily wear a burlap bag as clothing writing about philosophical ideas all day — instead of "wearing the purple" and having coins imprinted with his likeness on them.

"Wearing the purple" referred to the purple color — Tyrian purple — that represented royalty in ancient times. The purple dye was very difficult, laborious and costly to make. It took tens of thousands of sea snails (primarily found in the Mediterranean near the ancient seaport at Tyre) to produce even a small amount of this colorfast dye, so only the wealthy could afford entire garments of Tyrian purple.

Contrast that with Marcus's preference for wearing a brown, coarse-fibered hemp tunic. That gives a clear picture of what Marcus considered important in his life. It was not what was on the outside.

Pragmatic

Philosophy was never "ivory tower" type learning to me. It was always practical — how can it help me get from Point "A" to Point "B" most efficiently, with as few glitches in my thinking and emotions as possible.

Everything in my life was viewed through that lens. The philosophy of Stoicism was a way for me to see the world in a pragmatic way where the emotions did not overshadow the intellect, where they both worked hand in hand together, ideally in a state of balance. The closer my internal world was to a balanced state, the more efficient and effective my life was. And the more effective it was, the happier I became.

For Marcus, understanding how to make that process happen on a daily basis was his lifelong mission. He constantly strived towards improving his ability to manifest that type of life for himself.

Serious Demeanor

I recall taking my studies and tasks as a young boy very seriously — not just the study of philosophy, but all my studies, including oratory, mathematics, literature, ethics, physical exercise, and the fighting arts. I remember people commenting that I didn't smile enough.

After having had that memory, I later read historians describe my demeanor as "serious but friendly." And that the emperor Hadrian noticed the child's *gravitas* (seriousness, solemnity) and "noble bearing." Consequently, Hadrian nicknamed him *Verissimus* ("truest," "most genuine" in Latin), a nickname that later appeared on Roman coins.

Realist

Above all, I remember being a realist. I saw and — to the extent humanly possible — I accepted reality as it happened. That probably gave people around me the sense that I had an "air," almost an extra level of seriousness, that was noticeable. I was not quite robotic, but not as emotional as others perhaps.

Saw Anger as a Weakness

As I similarly remember when I was Richard and Frederick, Marcus saw anger as a weakness, and equanimity and balance as strengths. This might also have been incorrectly interpreted as Marcus being nonemotional.

Integrity, Fairness and Ethics

Many historians cite Marcus's commitment to truth and integrity, as well as his "disdain for duplicity." This is a trait I have embodied from even before I was Marcus — seeing my word as a duty, an ethical responsibility to be upheld.

Historians tell us that since he felt Marcus was too young, the emperor Hadrian adopted Antoninus Pius so that he would become emperor upon Hadrian's then impending death. He also made Antoninus's adoption and ascension conditional upon the latter adopting both Marcus and Lucius Verus. Consequently, when Antoninus died, it was expected that both Marcus and Lucius, who was eight years younger than Marcus, would become co-emperors.

There were many senior advisors and senators who were counseling Marcus to ignore that "formality" of following Hadrian's dying wishes. Instead, they advised Marcus to rule as the sole emperor himself. The Senate itself was even poised to confirm Marcus alone.

Nevertheless, Marcus felt it was his ethical duty to establish Lucius as his equal, in title at least, as "co-emperor" — to carry out Hadrian's dying wishes. So, he refused to take office unless the Senate also confirmed Lucius. The Senate acquiesced. It was the first time that Rome was ruled by two emperors at the same time.

My memory however is that while we were technically co-emperors, I was treated as the senior and therefore real emperor of Rome, even by Lucius himself. Not because I demanded it, but because of my age and experience.

Tragically, eight years later, Lucius died of what is now thought to have been smallpox. I grieved my stepbrother's death and had all the usual honors of a deceased emperor bestowed on him.

Compassion and Forgiveness

I had an interesting reaction when I learned of the following story several years ago.

During Marcus's reign as emperor, Avidius Cassius, his general in the eastern part of the Roman Empire either lied or was incorrectly told that Marcus was dead. Consequently, Cassius claimed himself to be emperor. When his troops learned the falsity of this rumor about Marcus's death, Cassius was assassinated by his own men, who sent Cassius's head to Marcus as proof.

When I was recently reminded of this series of events, I remembered how distraught I was 2,000 years ago at hearing of Cassius's murder. I respected and liked him. And I was looking forward to pardoning him and moving on from this unfortunate incident.

I remember not caring whether he had been lied to or whether he invented the falsehood himself. I was ready and willing to put it behind us. Again, both my pragmatism for respecting and valuing his military genius, coupled with my compassion for him as a close colleague (who was either misguided by another or himself) superseded his transgression to me and the Empire. Many others had done much worse over the history of the Empire. Many had gone unpunished and had even helped the Empire succeed in ways otherwise unimaginable. That is how I saw it.

At the very least, I wanted to give him an opportunity to explain to me what had happened, sitting calmly in person with me.

Moreover, historians tell us that Marcus had all of Cassius's correspondence burned, presumably to protect Cassius's co-conspirators, as well as Marcus's wife Faustina's reputation. While hard to substantiate given the conflicting 2nd century evidence, Faustina was reported to have taken many lovers, including Cassius. She died that same year in 175 A.D. at age 45, probably by natural causes from disease as her lack of immunity to the many viruses rampant outside of Rome where she normally lived may have caught up with her.

While our personalities were polar opposites — her enjoying the life as an aristocrat and all the pomp that went with it contrasted with my eschewing the fancy life and much preferring to be quiet and even alone sometimes — news of her death brought tears to my eyes because I know how conflicted Faustina was. She had been through a lot. Aside from the stress of being ordered by her father Antoninus (who was my stepfather) into an arranged marriage with me, the tragedy of death visited her many times as a mother. Fourteen or fifteen children were birthed and more pregnancies ended in miscarriages, with eight or nine of the children dying before age 10. Only five children lived past 10 years old. That takes its psychoemotional toll on any woman in any era.

Sexual Desire

I was not inactive when it came to having lovers outside of my marriage to Faustina, including after she died. I preferred quieter women compared to her feisty and flamboyant self. Not much is said about this, perhaps because historians want to protect Marcus's reputation as such a good emperor. But the reality is that while sexual desire did not drive Marcus — and he wrote specifically about how it was not a driver for him — he was not a celibate. Not being driven by sex along with the ability to choose to be celibate at times does not preclude the co-existence of the person's ability to also enjoy engaging in sexual activities.

Protection of Children

As much as I respected and felt a great deal of gratitude for the opportunities that the emperor Hadrian created for me as he groomed me from a very young age to succeed him,

I absolutely abhorred his propensity for pedophilia. Hadrian was a well-known pedophile and had many young boy lovers. It was allowed under Roman law, so he was not alone in his practice and proclivity.

Nevertheless, even though Roman culture was very tolerant of this choice by its adults, I found it reprehensible and spoke openly about my feelings about it. I felt that children should be protected from adults' sexual advances. It was wrong to me for adults to take advantage of the naïveté and curiosity of children, or to bribe them with various forms of gifts that most children would be susceptible to.

One of the many things I loved, and publicly praised, about my stepfather Antoninus Pius when he ascended to the throne upon Hadrian's death, was his immediate change of the law in this area. One of Antoninus's first acts as emperor was to make pedophilia a violation of Roman law.

Dislike of Gladiatorial Fights

As I distinctly recall from my memories as Richard, Frederick and Sitting Bull, I greatly disliked unnecessary violence — especially if it was just for the sake of show and entertainment, as with the gladiator games in Rome or jousting tournaments of the 12th century. This may sound odd for someone who was involved in so many wars and combat on the battlefields, however many of my traits have been deemed enigmatic. Nevertheless, while enigmatic, they seem to co-exist.

Historians tell us that Marcus disliked the gladiator fights that regularly occurred in the Colosseum. He understood that he had to go for political reasons in order to be seen by the general population as a participant in their favorite pastime. But while Marcus attended in person, he was not there in spirit.

He sat as usual in the emperor's box which was centrally situated so everyone in the Colosseum could see him. However, he surrounded himself with his close friends and leaders from the government, and instead of watching the fights, they discussed business and philosophy.

Seeing their emperor leaning towards various members of the group in the box often engaged deeply in conversation, the crowd assumed Marcus and his colleagues were discussing their wagers on the gladiator fights, just like the rest of the 50,000 captivated by the fighting on the arena floor. Little did they know what was actually going on — again, emblematic of an enigmatic personality.

Religious and Artistic Tolerance

Similar to my memories as Richard and Frederick, Marcus was reportedly very tolerant of the wide variety of religious beliefs present in the Empire, including those practiced right in his front yard, Rome. He also allowed artistic expressions that explicitly criticized him and his policies while he was emperor. Written critiques, speeches by his critics and theatrical performances by actors who disagreed with Marcus's views and governing actions were allowed to be, without any retribution. Contemporary writers have said that many of the emperors who preceded Marcus would have quickly had those guilty of such affronts whisked off and made to disappear forever.

I recall being relatively unaffected by how I was viewed by the masses, at least on a day-to-day basis. All I could do was to do my best to govern, create laws and wage wars that would protect the Empire. Much like my clear memories when I was Frederick, I viewed myself when I was Marcus as a "trustee" of the people, meaning my role was to protect them and their interests. Not to aggrandize my own. I took that role seriously.

I had a neutral attitude towards the early Christians as a group. I did not recognize them as teaching anything significantly different from the many other religious sects that existed then. They most certainly did not rekindle any memories of what I had learned from Jesus. At the same time, I did not see Christians as a threat to the Empire as some others did. They simply fell into the larger grouping of the many religious sects that I expressly promoted tolerance of by others. That included my encouragement of forbearance by the leaders of the Senate towards all religious groups. The persecution of the early Christians had been initiated by Nero, the emperor of Rome about one hundred years before Marcus.

Chapter 21

Personality

Richard the Lionheart

1157-1199

Richard the Lionheart, or Richard I, was born in Oxford, England at Beaumont Palace on September 8, 1157, the third son of Eleanor of Aquitaine and Henry II.

Bond Between Mother and Son

Richard was raised by his mother in Aquitaine, a region in southwestern France. Aquitaine became an English possession when Eleanor married Henry, who was King of England.

I recall being very close to my mother. Consistent with this, historians also record that of her five sons she birthed from Henry, Richard was her favorite. She called him "the great one." I remember she secured for me the best tutors in Aquitaine. Moreover, we are told that throughout most of his life (she outlived him) she tutored him in the art of politics, about which she was extremely skilled.

Philosophy and the Classics

Historians also have recorded that Richard studied at what was called Eleanor of Aquitaine's "court of love" in Poitiers where the participants studied the classics. So, as I remember similarly studying when I was Marcus and Frederick, we are told that Richard also immersed himself in the works of Plato and other Greek philosophers.

Moreover, as I recall exercising later in my life as Richard, and as I recall when I was Frederick and Sitting Bull, it is recorded that in addition to studying the classics at this court of love, we were also encouraged and taught how to revere, respect and protect women as valuable members of our culture, not merely as property. Many think that it was here that the code guiding the behavior of knights and chivalry, that subsequently became the norm throughout Europe, was born.

Love of French Language and Culture

My first love was France. I was raised there by a French-born mother who adored me. As I said, I remember how very close we were as mother and son. She was literally Richard's "life coach" his entire life. Consequently, his emotional bond with France was both wide and deep, personal and national.

Thus it is no wonder that, similar to my recollections as Frederick, I was a Francophile and fluent in French. Historians tell us that Richard's French was so good and his English so poor that his English critics often sarcastically spoke of his poor diction and inability to speak it fluently.

Compassion, Forgiveness, Shrewdness

I recall this event pretty clearly, as well as who the other main character in this story is today. I remember the chase, the almost being killed, and the forgiveness and the subsequent friendship. The forgiveness is reminiscent of how I recall wishing I could have treated Cassius when I was Marcus. In the following story, I don't remember all the dates and minutiae of the details, but I will tell the story in its relative completeness, relying on historical records shared by respected professionals so as to give a more complete, easier-to-follow context for the traits being elucidated here.

There is a well-known story about Richard and William Marshal that adds valuable insight into Richard's sense of forgiveness, loyalty and shrewdness. This happened in the aftermath of what is known as the Great Revolt that had been started sixteen years earlier in 1173 by the Young Henry, one of Richard's brothers, who was upset with his father Henry II.

During one of Richard's many armed battles with his father, the 31-year old Richard found himself allied this time with the king of France in a dispute over the ownership of various French regions, and which of Henry's sons would be the heir to the English throne. After many years of warring, Henry was then in a hasty retreat having reluctantly set fire to his own beloved birth city of Le Mans to provide a fire barrier to slow down Richard's pursuing army. Undaunted by his father's attempts at slowing his chase, Richard galloped ahead of his knights on an especially fast steed in hot pursuit of his father — and in his haste to quickly join his own knights — leapt onto his horse without any armor, weaponless, wearing only his tunic.

Meanwhile, William Marshal, known then as "the greatest knight in the realm" because of his skill at winning almost every tournament he entered (he was a huge physical specimen and a cunning warrior), had been protecting the King's rear guard with a retinue of well-armed, mail-clad knights on horseback. When he saw Richard and his knights approaching, Marshal turned abruptly to defend the King and, with his lance positioned in killing mode, charged straight at the defenseless, unarmed Richard.

I remember crying out (something to this effect), "By God, Marshal, do not kill me! That would be wrong. I am unarmed." To which Marshal replied, "No, let the Devil kill you, for I won't!" And he plunged his lance into Richard's horse, killing it instead.

A few weeks later, Henry agreed to the terms demanded by Richard and Philip, King of France, including that Richard would be heir to the throne of England. Shortly thereafter, King Henry II — having been informed on July 5 that his other son John had joined Richard in supporting Philip — succumbed the next day to a fever and died on July 6, 1189.

William Marshal sent a messenger immediately to inform Richard of the king's death. I remember forgiving Marshal for what had happened earlier when I was unarmed, and feeling thankful to him for his generosity and compassion for not killing me when he easily could have.

After paying his respects to his father, while outside the chapel Richard summoned Marshal, reminding him pointedly that just a few days earlier he had almost killed Richard. Marshal replied, "If I had wanted to kill you, I could easily have done so." Richard smiled, "Marshal, you are pardoned, I bear you no malice."

As a result of Henry's death, Richard the Duke of Aquitaine was now lord of Normandy and Anjou. His coronation as the new king of England would take place on Sunday, September 3, 1189 in Westminster Abbey.

As thanks to Marshal for his sparing my life, I gave him several meaningful gifts:

Richard bestowed on the 43-year old William Marshal lands in Wales and Ireland, and a beautiful 17-year old heiress Isabel Clare. This made Marshal vastly rich overnight.

Moreover, through this treatment of Marshal, Richard accomplished several things simultaneously. He displayed his magnanimity and forgiveness to a recent foe, put on view his gifts of patronage for all to see, and showed kingly wisdom and shrewdness in winning over the most important knight in the Empire. By doing so, Richard clearly contrasted his own generosity, reliability and decisiveness with the opposite traits of his father Henry II.

Richard's relationship with William Marshal grew over the ensuing years during which Marshal became a trusted advisor. He was even named a member of the regency council, responsible for governing England while the monarch, Richard, was in the Holy Land on the Third Crusade from 1190-1192.

Another example of Richard's compassion and propensity for forgiveness is that one of his first acts after his father died was to declare a general amnesty for political and social prisoners, publicly pointing out the fact that many men had been imprisoned purely for opposing his father. In contrast to his father, Richard wanted to demonstrate and emphasize justice rather than despotism as England's new ruler.

Generosity

I recall demonstrating similar acts of generosity when I was Marcus, Frederick and Sitting Bull. Although I do not recall this story about my wet nurse when I was Richard, I thought it was a telling one that historians have recorded because it not only showed this trait he possessed, but also how he expressed it so many years later, never forgetting her impact on his life.

Richard was reportedly very emotionally attached to his wet nurse, Hodierna, a native of St. Albans in England. Her own biological son, Alexander Neckam, was born on the same day as Richard. She breastfed both boys, although as heir to the throne, Richard was given the right breast, as it was thought to produce richer milk.

Given that both his father and mother were away for long periods of time in his infancy and early childhood, Richard's primary, almost sole source of emotional and physical support was Hodierna. She was his nanny and maternal figure, as an infant and young child. His care was literally in her hands — his very life in fact. And in that culture, had he died, she would have been held fully responsible.

When he became king, Richard never forgot her love and care for him those twenty-five years earlier. Consequently, he bestowed great riches upon her, and she became very wealthy. She is the only known wet nurse in history to have a town named after her. West Knoyle in Wiltshire was formerly known as Knoyle Hodierne.

Musician and Songwriter

I recall being poetically and musically inclined when I was Frederick, and historians record that Richard similarly was a supporter of music and the arts. He played the harp and was a songwriter himself. He was also very generous in his support of poets. While he was imprisoned in Austria being held hostage for ransom on his way back from the Crusade, he played his harp and wrote poetry in his room.

Verbal Acumen

It was said that Richard could "parry and thrust with his words as well as he could with a sword." He could be verbally sharp-worded and debate with great skill. And his style was generally conversational often described as "half bantering, half joking, half serious."

I recall this down-to-earth verbal style of communication as helping me in gaining the trust of my troops when I led them on the Third Crusade, as well as aiding me in the many negotiations I was involved in as King of England.

Decision Maker

Weighing all the options, thinking through their respective consequences, then choosing a path and executing on it was a process that was what I would call "just how I am wired." Being decisive in my decision making was just normal for me as Simon, Marcus, Richard, Frederick and Sitting Bull. That is how I remember it. It never felt out of the ordinary to me. In fact, I have often seen others over the millennia struggle at making decisions, and I have quizzically wondered why. My thinking after going through the above steps was always, "Ok, now that I have executed on the decision, let's see what's next and if I have to make an adjustment or not. I will not know whether I need to unless I make the initial decision."

I also recall that my ability to make those choices without excessive delay, in a confident manner, led some to perceive me as arrogant. I of course did not see myself that way. I thought I was just being practical, quick-minded and somewhat sure of myself, but never flaunting it in another's face. If I had flaunted it, to me that would have been arrogant.

To use some of the historian's words, Richard was known for being an "exceptionally decisive and quick thinker." This "mental strength and confidence in his decision making was sometimes interpreted by others as arrogance." However, contemporary writers who observed Richard's behavior first-hand chalked up those negative assessments of Richard as merely the comments of "those who tend to dither and waiver in their thinking and decisions."

Seeing the 'Fool For a Fool'

As I remembered when I was Simon Peter, I was skeptical of even those who claimed to be spiritual teachers. And I recall learning from Jesus how to refine my discernment skills in assessing other people's clarity of thought.

Similarly, historians have said of Richard that he never made the classic mistake of "confusing the half intelligent with the intelligent." The phrase used often in this context since the 1500's — "He didn't suffer fools gladly" — applied to Richard perfectly.

Nor did he ever "confuse earnestness with profundity." He clearly saw right through the person who merely stated things with brashness and conviction, trying to fool those within earshot that what that person was saying was meaningful or profound. And it is said that he called that out many times whenever he saw it.

Quick-Witted Sense of Humor

I recall exercising my sense of humor and sarcasm when I was Sitting Bull in a very similar way to the following story that historians have recorded about Richard.

Richard believed in putting the clergy in its place occasionally. The well-known preacher Fulk of Neuilly once

After the Afterlife

publicly scolded Richard for having three "daughters" — *Superbia, Luxuria, and Cupiditas* (pride, avarice and sensuality). He suggested that Richard would never receive the Grace of God as long as they remained by his side.

Richard thought a moment, then replied, "I have already given these daughters away in marriage. *Pride* I gave to the Templars, *Avarice* to the Cistercians, and *Sensuality* to the Benedictines." The Templars were an elite fighting force of knights as well as a religious order, and the Cistercians were a Catholic religious order of monks and nuns that had branched off from the Benedictines, another monastic order. I am sure those groups did not find this joke at their expense at all funny. However, it is a good example of the verbal ability that I recall having: to be able to incisively cut to the core and strike at the heart of someone, or in this case a group, if I wanted to.

Sexual Appetite Yet With Celibate Capability

The more astute historians researching and reporting without a religious or sexual orientation agenda seem to have most accurately captured the more nuanced sexual "personality" of Richard. I recall having had the unique ability — unlike most of the male population — of having a fondness for sex with at times a large appetite, yet the ability to go without for long periods and still maintain my inner balance.

Very similar to my recollections as Marcus, Frederick and Sitting Bull, I enjoyed it, could indulge in it, but did not live for it. I have read that Richard enjoyed many women throughout his life, including many women outside his arranged marriage to Berengaria.

Yet at the same time, I could be celibate, either by choice… or by forced circumstance, as in the case of my imprisonment for over a year when captured by Duke Leopold of Austria and the Holy Roman Emperor Henry VI of Germany, while I was on the return trip from the Third Crusade. I recall that unjust imprisonment, thinking, "Ha! You think you can get to my psyche by just locking me up? I actually enjoy solitude sometimes!"

Their imprisonment and ransoming of me was a clear violation of the "you cannot imprison a crusader on his way back from the crusades" rule as set out by the Pope. Nevertheless, the opportunity to hold Richard as hostage, ransoming his freedom to the highest bidder was too tempting to pass up.

There are many stories about Richard's extramarital exploits, although I do not have clear recollections of them. None of this seems surprising to me, however. Richard did not have a personality that was easily pigeonholed as absolutely this or that. Even with his love of sex, he could also abstain at will.

Extreme Sorrow

There are numerous accounts of Richard expressing sorrow over the loss of life as an inevitable outcome of wars.

Before I knew of this factoid about him (I had not started reading much about him until 2014), about fourteen years ago right after my girlfriend and I had been intimate, in that more open state emotionally and psychically, I spontaneously started sobbing. Still lying together and now crying freely, almost uncontrollably, I described my feeling intense sorrow of having been responsible for the deaths of so many thousands of people during the Third Crusade — on both sides, the crusaders as well as the Saracens. Not only the soldiers' deaths themselves, but perhaps even more significantly, I was sobbing over having caused so much grief in tens of thousands of lives of their relatives.

At that moment, I was envisioning the dead soldiers' spouses, children, grandparents, siblings, friends and acquaintances all suffering great emotional distress over the sudden loss of their loved ones. I felt a deep current of remorse wash over me, again and again. Waves of sorrow combined with feeling my own grief at having caused so many losses by my actions in that lifetime.

Disciplinary Code

As Marcus, Frederick and Sitting Bull, I recall being quite able to get my troops into "fighting shape." My input was less necessary in Rome because we already had a several hundred year tradition of high level military training in place, but the other ones benefited from my personal input and creation of disciplinary rules that helped our fighting forces excel.

I recall that when I was Richard, I had to access this skill for maintaining troop discipline and morale. This was no small task in the Middle Ages when full-time, well-organized and trained armies were not the norm. The knights were of course trained, but they only constituted a small percentage of the 20,000 troops who traveled with me from England to the Holy Land in the Third Crusade. The rest of the force was mostly made up of former farmers, criminals, and all manner of the mass population who wanted to have their sins forgiven by God (as promised by the Pope), their taxes ignored, or their debts magically made to disappear. So, you can imagine how unruly a group this would be.

Richard's "ability to maintain discipline among that huge motley group," that set sail on large barge-like ships bound for the adventures of the Third Crusade, "was impressive." Most of them did indeed view this simply as an adventure, an odyssey.

Most of them had never been outside of their small hamlet or village, never mind outside of England, or in a foreign country where the natives did not speak the same language, eat the same food or wear the same clothes as they did. And...never mind that they were going there to fight a "holy war," sanctioned by God himself.

But even those thoughts were secondary to 99% of the troops. Most of them were just looking forward to raping, pillaging and killing — not necessarily in that order. They fantasized about coming back to England as rich men with sacks full of gold objects and rare gems, the "spoils of war." And those who were married were looking forward to having as many extramarital affairs as possible, while those who were still virgins, were looking forward to ending that drought.

That was the type of crowd of hoodlums that Richard had to manage. In order to do so, he created one of the first naval disciplinary codes.

The disciplinary part and the extremes to which I had to go to maintain order, I remember. The details, however, I do not remember. So I will share what historians have recorded about that disciplinary "code."

This code illustrates both Richard's tactics and attitude towards managing these 20,000 rowdy men on the 216 ships while on the long shipboard trip from England to the Holy Land. Granted, some of the measures exercised to maintain acceptable behavior if used today would be considered draconian.

For example, if someone murdered another member of this holy expedition during the trip, the killer would be buried or thrown overboard while tied to the victim's body — buried if the murder was on land, thrown overboard if it was done at sea. If it was proven by lawful witnesses that a man drew a knife on another, his hand was cut off. If a man punched another without drawing blood, he was immersed three times in the sea, more times if he drew blood. The penalty for abusive or blasphemous language was one ounce of silver for each occasion. Any man caught stealing, had his head shaven, was tarred and feathered, then put ashore at the first landfall. And so forth....

Richard felt that these extreme disciplinary methods were necessary to manage his troops, many of whom were from the underbelly of society. Most were not there for "religious" reasons at all, nor did they come from towns or villages where there were any criminal laws. They were used to "running free," having their way in whatever manner suited them, with little or no consequences to their actions.

Richard's code of behavior for his men may understandably horrify us in the 21st century, but some of the most common situations that the regular person in 12th century Europe had to deal with everyday would horrify us today even more so than these draconian disciplinary methods. Take for example the lack of toilets or plumbing, how close the cows were to the stream where you got your water to drink, how many people got murdered regularly at the local village tavern...to name just a few. All of the media outlets in 2023 combined could not have covered all the atrocities happening every day throughout 12th century Europe.

Richard's wisdom in establishing this code of conduct for his 20,000 troops was soon borne out. When the ships set ashore in Lisbon, Portugal for resupply, 700 of the men were arrested in one night. These so-called "soldiers of God" started a riot beating up the locals, targeting the worshippers of Judaism and Islam first. They then moved on to raping, murdering, pillaging, burning and gutting buildings, and trampling orchards. They plundered everything in sight in that one night. Fortunately for Richard, "the king of Portugal decided to only jail the offenders instead of hanging all of them, which would have been justified. The papal proscription against harming crusaders saved the 700 from the gallows they deserved."

Here is how I recall thinking about my disciplinary code at the time:

I felt that if you were stupid enough to contravene my very clear instructions to not fight with each other, that demonstrated such a minimal ability to make good enough choices to stay alive *outside* of a battle, that when that poor soul was *in* a battle, they would be killed almost immediately. So, in that way, my disciplinary methods — though arguably extreme — would teach these former drunkards, thieves and rapists quickly…or, they would lose their fingers or limbs by my "disciplinary hand." But at least I hadn't killed them outright, which would probably happen soon enough…for those stupid enough to transgress my rules more than once or twice, were probably the types who would end up killing each other before we arrived in the Holy Land.

I figured in a life or death situation, where one's own life was at stake, who would want such an undisciplined idiot guarding your flank? So, if my disciplinary rules that outlined a bare modicum of civil behavior for all of us to get to the Holy Land alive were too tough, then at least those "loose cannons" would be tossed overboard and not waste our food and water unnecessarily when the rest of us, who were committed to helping each other survive, got to the desert.

Caring For His Men and Their Lives

I remember as Marcus, Frederick, Sitting Bull and Richard that I was loathe to put my men in harm's way unnecessarily.

I protected them like they were my sons, trying my best to strategize a winning battle plan beforehand and preparing the troops for whatever that era's tactics and weaponry allowed.

Sure, I could be a tough disciplinarian of the troops, but I also made sure they were well taken care of — fed well, kept hydrated in the desert climate, and I was ever mindful of not using them as "pawns" simply for short-term tactical gain on the battlefield. Richard's troops knew that he valued their lives and that he took that into account in his meticulous battle planning during the campaign in the Holy Land.

They soon became well aware that this set Richard apart from other military leaders. They saw him work as hard as they did. I recall many times taking off my shirt to join them in building castle walls, digging wells, and other projects involving intense manual labor — sweating alongside them under the hot desert sun. At the initial battle and siege of Acre soon after we arrived in the Holy Land, as the Crusaders tried to take down the fortress's massive Maledicta Tower, "to set an example, Lionheart himself joined the demolition work, manhandling masonry while arrows zipped by his massive frame." Acre fell in July 1191, about a month after Richard's arrival.

I have crystal clear memories of being the first who rode into the battle at the point of the phalanx. Both Richard and his 1400-pound warhorse were suited up in their battle gear — exhorting his troops who doggedly and repeatedly followed him into the fray. Anyone who has ever witnessed a battlefield during any era of human history will tell you that there is nothing more inspirational than when your commanding general is at the "tip of the spear" in front of you leading the charge into the heart of the enemy horde. I wanted to demonstrate to my men that I did not shirk from the danger that I was putting them in, that

I readily joined alongside them in sharing that danger, and sought to divert that danger from them as much as I could by fighting first in front of them.

The Warrior Mentality

I distinctly recall not wanting to fight if we didn't have to. But if we had to, we would go "all out." No holding back.

If a given conflict needed to be resolved through fighting a war, then so be it. If that was the most effective, obvious or necessary means to resolve the conflict, okay. But I don't recall ever seeking it or "loving" it. I saw passionately engaging in the battle as a necessary evil of war. But the passion I expressed that may have been misinterpreted by only observing me on the outside was internally my passion for living, for staying alive. Not my passion for killing. From the outside however, that is very difficult to distinguish.

Said another way, I saw my passion for living as simply an expression of my pragmatic side. How could I get anything done, if I was dead?

However, if there was another means, through negotiations or other deal making, then I would pursue that with equal vigor. Historians have said that Richard "took every challenge seriously, planning carefully, and was not too proud to take advice from others or learn from his mistakes."

But above all, his so-called "love of war" as a necessary evil was always done with a purpose. Never cavalierly. Never unnecessarily. Never for personal gain.

I recall absolutely despising tournaments and jousts, sporting events that were popular in the Middle Ages, often held to showcase the hosting aristocrat's wealth and ability to "one-up" the neighboring lords. It was the Middle Age version of what I call the "Importance of Being Important." That is, "my jousts were fancier than your jousts…so there!"

It is true that they were a way for some "warrior type" men to channel their aggression and make money by winning tournaments. However, I always thought there could be better alternatives to making a living.

I viewed those tournaments as a childish adult version of how young boys often play and compete, except in this case it was being played out by grown barons and lords. These shows seemed like an impractical exercise in showiness to me. And moreover, I viewed it as a dangerous high risk sport where people could get unnecessarily killed. Again, the pragmatist in me coming out.

Here is another example that the historical records reveal to us about Richard's pragmatic view of the warrior mentality:

In England, when he became king, "he forbade his lords from waging war on each other whenever they felt like it, which had previously been their tradition. Again, this was another example of his practical side. War was not something to be taken lightly, only engaged in when necessary. That was Richard's stance on it. To avoid armed conflict whenever possible, he rigidly enforced laws and legal codes throughout England." From a practical standpoint, he saw that enforcement as an effective way of avoiding the incredible expense, both in terms of weaponry and loss of life and property, that people tended to overlook when they felt "wronged," and instead irrationally just lashed out.

"In the Zone" on the Battlefield

As far as the experience of being engaged on the actual battlefield, I have many visceral, visual and emotional memories from the 12th century.

A partial list includes the following.

Being "in the zone" and "seeing things before they happened" made me extremely effective as a warrior. Even though I was typically the first on horseback into the fray, I was never seriously wounded or killed on the battlefield.

I attribute this to the heightened sense of being in the present that may have come from the intense focusing of my mind in those life or death situations. I was able to anticipate the actions of others near me on the field of battle, before they had even fully moved, by intuiting or sensing their initial bodily movements or facial expressions. This was an automatic phenomenon, beyond thinking. I was spontaneously in that state of "being in the moment." Sometimes it seemed like I was almost "ahead of the moment."

Richard did not have a "blood lust" for killing, although it may have appeared as such to the uninitiated observer not used to experiencing first-hand battlefield chemistry and physiology. It was not a "blood lust" but an adrenaline rush that pushes all other thoughts out of one's mind except the primeval drive of the survival of the fittest. Otherwise, I would quickly be killed myself.

To those who have never experienced actual hand-to-hand combat it may understandably be misinterpreted as "loving to kill." This is often a mistaken impression gleaned by the naïve bystander. Those who may have been farmers tending the fields, while a very important job, have little idea what it is to be at their "life or death" moment hundreds of times in a matter of a compressed few minutes or hours — which can subjectively feel to the warrior in the midst of battle as if the "life or death" moment is happening every split second.

It is a very different "way of life." And it brings a very different sensibility to what war is, to what life and death are. It makes the wars that the townspeople may glorify and cheer about much less desirable when you have actually been on the battlefield, blood-splattered, wielding the ax or sword yourself, seeing your closest friends die all around you — like I have.

Anger Over the Execution of My Killer

After I died, I remember being extremely annoyed with my officers for contravening my express orders to not kill the boy who shot the crossbow bolt that accidentally killed me.

Interestingly, one wonders: had Saladin been prescient in telling Richard that his Achilles heel was engaging personally in military operations that did not need the king's attention or involvement, things that should better have been left to subordinates to do? Because on March 15, 1199, Richard went with his troops to besiege the castle of the rebellious Viscount of Limoges at Châlus-Chabrol, south of Limoges, France. The relatively small castle had no more than 40 defenders. Nevertheless, instead of delegating this minor operation, Richard stayed and directed the siege personally.

At dusk on March 29, Richard decided to take a stroll in the early evening air and shoot some bolts at the castle walls with his crossbow. It was more an exercise in target practice than anything else — after all, what could a relatively small wooden shaft with a metal tip do to a massive castle wall?

Being lazy that evening, I left my tent with just my shirt on, not even quickly donning my chain mail shirt over it — why carry the extra weight, I thought, I'm not going into battle, just having some fun shooting some bolts at the wall to see how good my aim still is. For protection, all he had was a large rectangular shield.

Way up on the castle parapet all alone stood the same boy who was often there around the same time each evening. He would routinely take occasional shots at the besiegers off in the distance just to annoy them, his token gesture of defiance — something that a teenage boy would do in almost any era, especially one who was not happy with what we were doing to his friends and family in their castle.

Richard was either not paying attention to how close the boy's bolts were coming or maybe he was fascinated that the young boy had the gumption to do this nightly ritual. For whatever reason — surprising everyone — one of the bolts buried itself in Richard's left shoulder.

Annoyed and probably embarrassed, Richard did not immediately ask one of his men to remove it. Instead he went back to his tent and tried to pull it out himself, carelessly snapping the wooden shaft leaving the iron barb buried in his shoulder, now making it even more difficult to remove. By the time the surgeon came, either because Richard had butchered the attempt to remove it himself and thus had created an even bigger wound, or perhaps because the surgeon could not see well enough in the dimly lit tent, the wound was a big mess by the time the bolt was finally removed.

But beneath the bandages the wound had already been invaded by *septicemia*, arguably the most common cause of death on the battlefields of the Middle Ages — and the bacterial infection caused blood poisoning which soon triggered sepsis. Gangrene developed and on April 6, the Tuesday before Palm Sunday, Richard the Lionheart took his last breath.

While he was on his deathbed, he forgave the boy who shot the bolt that killed him. Richard ordered his men not to kill the boy, who was horrified that he had wounded the king while playing what he thought was his evening "game" of annoying the besiegers. Nevertheless, once Richard was dead, his soldiers killed the boy anyway.

Was Richard's desire to bestow his forgiveness on the young lad akin to the forgiveness he had received himself 1200 years earlier? I wonder.

Friendship With Saladin?

We obviously had completely different religious, political and military interests during the crusades. However, I remember meeting with him a number of times in a tent in the middle of the desert, sitting with each other in person to discuss truces, treaties, and the like. A kinship developed. We developed a palpable, mutual regard for each other as warriors and as leaders of our people.

Saladin, the leader of the Saracens (whom we today call "Muslims") who was the Sultan of Egypt and Syria, recaptured Jerusalem in 1187, four years before Richard the Lionheart arrived to attempt to retake it on behalf of Christendom. It is not disputed that in his recapture of the Holy City, Saladin (Salah al-Din Yusuf ibn Ayyub was his full name, shortened by Westerners to "Saladin") spared the lives of thousands of the Christian inhabitants, allowing almost all of them to leave peacefully.

I remember respecting him and, in other less conflict-ridden times, we probably would have been friends. Saladin died of illness and exhaustion in his gardens in Damascus, just a few short months after he and Richard agreed on a truce in September 1192, ending the Third Crusade.

Falling Out With the Pope — Questions Authority

Richard decided to pen a three-year peace treaty with Saladin, leaving Jerusalem and returning to Europe because, among other reasons including the indefensibility of Jerusalem, he saw through the Pope's agenda. From a religious standpoint, the Pope could always argue that, notwithstanding the fact that all three of the main monotheistic religions — Judaism, Christianity and Islam — had their reasons for claiming Jerusalem as "their" holy city, he of course was the leader of Christianity. So even though there was great commonality among those three religions in terms of their beliefs in the ancient Biblical prophets, angels, divine guidance by one God, etc., and moreover that both Christianity and Islam viewed Jesus as a main religious figure, from the Pope's self-interested seat, Jerusalem and the surrounding Holy Land was primarily for Christians and therefore to be ruled by Christians only. This was the obvious publicly stated "Christian party line."

However, gradually over time, even after the Crusade, Richard began to see other ulterior motives harbored and exercised by Pope Innocent III. Perhaps one of the events that shed further light on the questionable intentions of the Pope were Richard's negotiations with the pontiff through Peter of Capua the Elder, the pontiff's slimy, obsequious, overreaching envoy, or "papal legate" (personal representative of the Pope to foreign nations).

In August 1198, the Pope sent his legate to France to arrange a peace accord or at least a five-year truce between the warring kings, Philip II of France and Richard I of England. During a meeting with Richard and William Marshal, Peter of Capua the Elder convinced Richard to agree to a conditional five-year truce. However, when he persisted in asking that Richard also release the Bishop of Beauvais, whom the king intensely hated, Richard lost his temper and threatened to castrate the legate. According to Marshal, the legate was visibly shaken.

I don't recall all of the above details, but I do recall having a series of negotiations with the "slimy" Peter of Capua and thinking that he was a logical extension of how the Pope himself would have conducted the negotiations, and thus it further lowered the Pope's esteem in my mind.

One noteworthy fact is that during the nearly two centuries that the nine crusades spanned, the many popes who oversaw Christendom for those 176 years were quite concerned about so many Christians killing each other in local battles and wars throughout Europe in the 12th and 13th centuries — kings fighting kings, dukes fighting dukes, barons fighting barons. The popes feared that the population of Christians might plummet if this continued unabated, especially over many decades for many generations.

So what better way to keep more Christians alive than to get them all excited to kill Saracens, "infidels" safely tucked far away from Europe across the sea in the Middle East? Sure, lots of Christians would still die, but at its worst it would still only be half the losses suffered, compared to them killing off their own "religious brothers and sisters" across Europe. Not adopting this strategy to get the lords to go kill off Saracens would have potentially resulted in twice as many Christians dying in senseless battlefield skirmishes across Europe, instead of half as many dying in the Holy Land. At least that's what the popes thought.

I'm not suggesting that was their primary motive. Of course, they were in fact the leaders of the Christian world so they did see Jerusalem and the surrounding Holy Land as theirs to rightly rule, along with the need to protect pilgrimages giving them safe passage to and from, as well as other political and religious objectives. So, whether or not the above concern over the potential killing of Christians by Christians was a primary motive of Pope Gregory VIII who ordered the Third Crusade, it was certainly one of the factors considered, one that Richard potentially saw as self-serving and which Richard questioned, "at what cost of loss of life"?

In any event, Richard was above all a thinker, and far from naïve. So it is safe to say that he was not impressed by the Pope's repeated demonstrable lack of ability to be "a good Christian," as shown by the pope's thoughts and actions.

And thus, I vowed to never be hoodwinked by a religious authority figure again, certainly not one claiming to be a Christian. From that moment on, the soul then known as Richard the Lionheart eschewed religious zealots, yet continued to encourage religious tolerance.

Chapter 22

Personality

Frederick the Great

1712-1786

Connection With His Soldiers and Citizenry

Perhaps one of the most intense emotional memories from this lifetime is my "deep connection on a relational level" with the many people I encountered throughout my 74-year life as Frederick.

It is interesting that this is my strongest type of memory as Frederick — an emotional and relational one. Because he is typically known by historians as a great military strategist, leader of his country's army, and expansionist of Prussia's borders through wars with the surrounding nations, leading Prussia to become arguably the most powerful, respected and feared nation in Europe at the time.

Yet my memories are more focused on my relationships with so many people who represented a wide array of the Prussian society at the time — my family and close friends, my fellow government servants, my soldiers (officers and "rank and file" alike), and my citizenry from all walks of life. Frederick had an uncanny ability to recall names and faces, as well as the background stories of that individual.

It is noteworthy that Frederick was named "the Great" by his people, the people he ruled as their king. He didn't think of himself as "better than" them. In fact, he is known for having stated many times that his role was as a "trustee" of the people.

That means that I felt that I was "in *their* service." My role as king was to help nurture and protect them, to do whatever I could to improve their lives whether it be through my financial infrastructure decisions, my military exploits, or my promotion of religious tolerance and immigration. In all cases, I served at the pleasure of the people. While of course, I had inherited the crown as was customary in the cultures of that time, I did not view myself as anything other than "a servant of the people." I was not in the role of being their leader for me to take advantage of them for myself or those around me, but instead to do my best to help improve the lives of the entire population of our nation.

I viewed my role as a responsibility, a duty. Not a gift.

In fact, there is a funny quote from Frederick who said, "A crown is just a hat that lets the rain in." But it is a revealing statement, showing that he viewed himself as just another man. Not better than the others around him. Perhaps more fortunate due to the family into which he was born, but not better.

Consistent with that self-perception, on the battlefield he wore essentially the same uniform as all of his troops, not one that would indicate his role as supreme commander. He did not flaunt his regal status, and in fact downplayed it. Even in formal attire later in life, he wore a soldier's tunic and one decoration, the Order of the Black Eagle Breast Star. On it was engraved a motto in Latin ("SUUM CUIQUE") that guided Prussian kings for over 200 years: "To each according to their merit." It expressed that only accomplishments that were earned were to be rewarded, and by contrast, corruption and favoritism were to be shunned.

Here is another telling example that I read about a few years ago from a collection of actual letters written by and to Frederick in the late 1700's. When Frederick was in what we would today call semi-retirement in his late 60's to early 70's, meaning he was still running the country but not engaging personally in aggressively expanding the political and geographic borders of his country, he received a letter from an elderly farmer and his wife. They described in detail their financial plight, having lost almost all their money in market shifts in the prices of livestock and crops, actions that they had no control over, that were much bigger than they were and which they could not withstand. They were thus unable to support themselves or repay their debts.

Frederick wrote them a letter and sent them enough money from the national funds so they could pay off their debts and live modestly for the rest of their lives. Not only did I resonate with his compassion for this unknown couple living in rural Prussia, but primarily I was struck by the core content, the body of his letter.

He proceeded to "teach" them, even then in the twilight of their lives, instructing them to manage this money carefully, that it would be their sole grant from him and the country's coffers, and that they would have to spend it wisely and frugally for the rest of their lives. But that they could now relax and enjoy their remaining years here on Earth.

It was this caring for his people for which Frederick was widely known among his people. His citizenry certainly did not miss noticing this aspect of his personality.

Another story that appears in that book of letters penned by Frederick himself is about an incident that occurred while his coachmen were driving him through the farmlands simply touring the countryside one day. Frederick, who was in his 70's at the time, did this often as a way to relax in his waning years.

As they passed an elderly man tending to his garden outside his modest cottage along the road, Frederick instructed his coachmen to stop. He looked at the man in the garden and called out his name and said, "Is that you?" The man, hard of hearing, paused and turned. Then he recognized that it was, of course, the king's carriage. And he said, "Yes, it is I, your majesty."

It turns out that Frederick had recognized one of his former, now quite elderly, army officers who was out tending his garden. Frederick got out of his carriage, gave him a big hug and they chatted about old times together. Frederick listened intently as this one-time officer, whom he viewed not only as his former military colleague, but also more importantly as his friend, filled him in on his life since retiring from the army. His wife soon joined them with some light food she had made, as this couple spent precious memorable moments laughing and sharing stories with their king along the side of that country road.

It is this informal, caring and "connecting" side to Frederick's personality that earned him the equally informal yet loving nickname by his people, "Ole Fritz." While I do not recall all the details of these stories, I do very much remember the emotional feelings I had in those many instances that these few stories elucidate.

Strategic, Practical, Decisive, Common Sense

The following three simple examples sum up how practical but strategic Frederick was in his military successes on the battlefield. These traits are also exemplified in the lives of Simon Peter, Marcus, Richard, and as I'll discuss next, Sitting Bull. All of them were exceedingly strategic, practical and decisive, with common sense that was striking, even to the casual observer.

The Ramrod

The primary infantry weapon of 18th century Europe was the musket. It was a single shot rifle that could be loaded and fired by a well-trained soldier between two to three times a minute. The ramrod was a device used with muzzleloading firearms to push the projectile up against the propellant (mainly black powder). The ramrod was used with weapons such as muskets and cannons. It was usually held in place in a notch underneath the musket barrel.

The infantry weapon of the Royal Prussian Army was the "Potzdam musket," manufactured in 1723 and improved upon in its 1740 model, the year Frederick took the throne. Frederick introduced the innovative *iron* ramrod and then later the *reversible* ramrod with a conical shape on both ends, which increased the firing efficiency — and confidence — of his infantry.

By contrast, every infantryman of their British, Austrian, French, Russian, and Swedish counterparts used a *wooden* ramrod. A narrow rod three-eighths of an inch in diameter, about 35-40 inches long, it was prone to breaking in the stress of battle. Obviously, a musket that could not be loaded with a musket ball quickly — or even at all — became useless as a rifle, and only good for attaching a bayonet for hand-to-hand combat. An explosive, powerful, projectile-launching handheld weapon could essentially be relegated to being simply a long knife, often in an instant in the midst of the battlefield mêlée. This was the fate of many of the infantrymen who fought against Frederick's more well-equipped army.

Why didn't the other European countries invent or immediately adopt the iron ramrod? Because it was more expensive. It required a more organized infrastructure to make them en masse, whereas a wooden ramrod could be made by any farmer or non-professional who had decent carpentry skills.

So my thinking was: why not spend a few extra *thalers* (the currency of Prussia) per infantryman to 1) potentially save his life, so fewer men would be lost in battle, and 2) to win the battles and potentially the war. To me, the calculus was easy, a no-brainer. I never understood the hesitation to adopt this new technology by the neighboring nations who finally did so, but much later when it was too late to be meaningful in their battles with Prussia.

Persistence in Battle

The second example was Frederick's persistence in battle, and his willingness to adjust his strategy, making what we now call "in-game adjustments." This battlefield skill is something I remember he shared with Marcus, Richard and Sitting Bull. Consistent with that was his "stick-to-it-ness" during and after battles — battles that often seemed to many on the battlefield to have been already lost.

There are examples of even his own troops thinking they had been defeated, where Frederick said, "No." He would nevertheless pursue the enemy who also had assumed victory and frequently was already settling into their "post-victory relaxed mode" — tending to their wounded, collecting bodies from the battlefield, or getting something to eat.

Frederick would rally his troops, launch a surprise attack from a different angle, and reengage in battle. He would often catch his opponents completely by surprise, and rout them in the process, emerging as the final victor at the end of the day.

What is the moral of those events?

It's simple. Don't give up until you know for sure that you have lost. Never let your guard down if your enemy is nearby enough to counterattack. Finally, taking risks and thinking "out of the box" is part of being a triumphant military leader, or of being a successful leader of any kind.

"Practice Makes Perfect"

The third example was the superior efficiency and discipline of the Prussian regiments, enabling them to move around the battlefield with a speed, maneuverability and orderliness that no other European army could match. They were also known to be able to fire up to five musket shots per minute compared to up to three shots for other European armies.

This was based simply on repetitive drills.

Again, I always thought it was not "rocket science" to deduce that the time spent with the troops in drilling maneuvers — over and over again until it became second nature to them and their superior officers — would pay back a multifold return on investment on the battlefields. After all, that is the time when I needed to move my troops in unison or break them up into separate units, whichever approach seemed to be tactically advantageous in that moment. But it had to be done swiftly and without any confusion by either my senior leaders on the field or my infantrymen under their command. In those moments, every minute counted and being in the wrong location at the wrong time could result in our own cannons firing directly on our position by mistake. Moreover, I preached to my officers that swift and exact alignment and realignment of troops achieved a "multiplied force effect" during a battle.

I suspect that the only thing holding back the troops from the other countries' armies from drilling to the same extent as Frederick demanded was sheer laziness. I could not imagine what else it might be. And I repeat myself, but it bears repeating, that Frederick, even at the young age of 28, felt that the lives of his men were so valuable, not only as humans with souls but also as weapons of war to win battles, that this investment of time spent on drilling maneuvers, as well as musket and cannon loading practice, and other training was more than worth the effort.

His enthusiasm and innate knowingness that this time and energy would pay off multifold down the road was shared by his senior officers in the field. And that enthusiasm trickled down to the newest recruits.

That enthusiasm and confidence alone eventually put Frederick's troops well ahead of the other competing armies in Europe often before they even stepped onto the battlefield. It also cemented the love of his troops for him that existed not only during their lifetimes in the 18th century, but also beyond as was described in my brochure example of their interjecting the Prussian blue uniform shade into the color palette.

As a related side note, in 1777, one of Frederick's former General Staff, Baron Friedrich von Steuben was recommended by the French minister of war to Benjamin Franklin who passed the word on to George Washington. In 1778 at Valley Forge, Washington invited von Steuben to train the ragtag Continental Army in Prussian military techniques. Based on his successful efforts at Valley Forge, Washington recommended that von Steuben be named Inspector General of the Continental Army and Congress approved the appointment. Von Steuben, who did not speak English, then drafted a military drill manual in French which was translated into English by Alexander Hamilton and Nathanael Greene. In this capacity, von Steuben propagated his methods, with Congress's endorsement, throughout the Patriot forces by circulating his "Blue Book" in 1779 (so named because of the blue paper that was the only available paper to print it on), officially entitled "Regulations for the Order and Discipline of the Troops of the United States." These Prussian drill techniques taught by von Steuben were far more advanced than those of other European armies, which gave Washington's army a decided advantage in their subsequent war efforts against the British in the Revolutionary War.

No Physical Blows in Training

I remember being a team builder. Here is a good example.

Yet another striking example of his wisdom of how to train and manage troops in preparation for success on the battlefield was his forbidding physical blows in training, except in extreme circumstances. He recognized the need for his men to have absolute and instantaneous obedience to their superior officers along with the inculcation of trust among their comrades in arms.

By disallowing actual fist fights that could have easily erupted into brawls during heated training exercises, Frederick helped the men maintain a sense of brotherhood and camaraderie, an intangible on the battlefield that is impossible to measure the value of in quantifiable terms, yet when it is lacking, the tragic results in the aftermath are sadly calculated often by the number of dead bodies of the losing army.

Use of On-Site Witnesses

Another demonstration of his creativity and astuteness was his finding an old man who lived near the site of a previous battle and who remembered it in great detail. Frederick had him describe what had happened, so the king could learn from the past mistakes of other military commanders who had previously fought on that very same field.

Love of Music and Languages, Independent-Minded

Interestingly, similar to Richard the Lionheart who ruled 600 years earlier, Frederick the Great was a Francophile. Neither king was inclined to speak the native tongue of the countries they each ruled. Both much preferred speaking French. Moreover, both kings were sometimes openly ridiculed by their critics at failing miserably in their ability to speak their own country's language with anything more than a labored attempt at fluency.

Frederick chose not to speak German but instead to speak and write in French almost all the time, notwithstanding the fact that he was king of a German-speaking country. He was much more prolific and fluent in French than German, speaking German with a noticeable non-German accent, yet speaking French flawlessly. Frederick was multilingual, also versed in English, Spanish, Italian and Portuguese. He even secretly learned Latin when he was a young prince disregarding the orders of his tyrannical father, King Frederick William, who forbade it.

In addition, he (like Richard) was especially fond of "speaking" through music. Both men were musically inclined, but Frederick was even more prolific. He both composed music for and performed on his flute. The depth of Frederick's talent is reflected in the following: he wrote 121 sonatas for flute, four flute concertos, a symphony and various arias. He performed often in his palace of *Sanssouci* (which means "without worry" in French) along with his chamber ensemble to audiences of Europe's dignitaries, nobility and leading philosophers of the era — Bach, Voltaire and many others. His original flute still exists in the family collection at the Hohenzollern Palace, the ancestral home of the Hohenzollern royal family, which owns the instrument.

Frederick practiced his flute — made of silver, ebony and ivory — up to four hours a day. It is reportedly still in perfect condition, yet was made in 1750 by his flute teacher, Johann Joachim Quantz. In 2009, it was played for the first time in 230 years at the Usedom Festival whose theme that year was Prussia.

Youthful Insight and Independent Thought

As I remember with Marcus, Richard and Sitting Bull, Frederick was also an insightful youth who thought independently from birth. Like Marcus and Richard, he was enamored with reading a wide variety of books starting at a very young age building a broad base of knowledge across a wide range of subjects.

At 14, young prince Frederick was appointed Major of the Potsdam Grenadiers. He was physically tiny at that age, under four feet tall (he would only be 5'7" as an adult), very thin, with 2 enormous blue eyes. The prince was required to go out, mingle and engage in society, had to pretend to smoke and drink, both habits he loathed to the end of his days.

Still 14 years old, he began creating his own library, the catalog of which still exists written in his own handwriting. He collected books on mathematics and science, history, art, music, politics, translations from the classics — practically all were written in French, even the German histories. The young boy longed to become a French poet. He made French jokes, grew his hair long, even combing it in the French style of the day.

Here is a funny story revealing how widespread the knowledge was about his abusive father:

Frederick's father, King Frederick William, took his young son to a barber ordering him to shear his "disgusting" locks. Frederick cried while the kind barber snipped and snipped — his scissors making all the right noises for the king to hear but barely cutting anything at all — then he moistened the hair with enough water so he could flatten it out and make it *appear* like he had done something. However, he had left enough so that later Frederick could coif it up again, obviously when his father, the king, was not present.

At 19, Frederick created his first blueprint of the political foreign policy for Prussia in the form of a long letter to several elder guardians. These generals, who were sympathetic to Frederick's plight, nevertheless were ordered by King Frederick William to guard the young prince in his imprisonment after he got caught plotting to escape to England from the oppressive life imposed by his father. Frederick was imprisoned in the Fortress of Küstrin from September 2 to November 19, 1731, and exiled from court until February 1732. The Holy Roman Emperor intervened on his behalf and ordered his father to release him.

Frederick's deep interests in music, philosophy, and the classics, coupled with his contempt for hunting animals simply for the sake of killing, enraged his oppressive, machismo father who thought those interests were decadent and unmanly. Frederick hated hunting so much, thinking it was "cruel and dumb," that his father would often discover that he had escaped from the hunt, finding him talking with his mother in her carriage, or in a forest glade playing his flute.

Of course, it didn't help matters that the young prince had long hair, wore exotic clothes, thought and spoke in French, and openly pretended to hate anything to do with the army. All of this further infuriated his father who publicly called him effeminate.

Doesn't Frederick sound like a "child of the 1960's"? A rebel, contrarian, anti-authoritarian, non-rule follower, long-haired iconoclast — all would be accurate ways of describing the young prince Frederick.

Even as a youth, he had icy self-control. Frederick never flew into rages, like his father did multiple times a day. And he somehow managed to receive his father's physical blows and verbal insults with an air of maddening indifference — the ultimate in rebuffs.

The young prince and heir to the throne was treated with intolerable cruelty by his father, as was everyone in the household. He was beaten for being thrown off a bolting horse and for wearing gloves in cold weather. Not only was cruelty delivered by the king in words, but also in flying objects at one's head and torso…dishes, bowls, silverware, etc. Terror reigned in the house — Frederick's mother the Queen, who was almost always pregnant (14 times), cried every day.

Devotion to His Wife and Their Arranged Marriage

As was the tradition, custom and practice of the times, marriages of the more well-to-do were typically arranged by the parents. The underlying objective was to create a better business or political relationship between the two families, and depending on how influential the families were, perhaps even influence world politics. This was the attempt by Frederick's father in having his son marry Elisabeth Christine of Brunswick-Wolfenbüttel-Bevern.

Soon after Frederick's failed attempt to escape to England from his father's tyrannical and abusive relationship — where he was cruelly forced to witness the beheading of his friend and tutor, Hans Hermann von Katte, on November 6, 1730 who had aided in that escape attempt — the Crown Prince was ordered by his father to marry Elisabeth Christine, who was the niece of Elisabeth Christine of Brunswick-Wolfenbüttel, wife of the Holy Roman Emperor Charles VI. The marriage was obviously a betrothal purely of political strategy, not love, between the 17- and 20-year old.

The best sales pitch the King could give Frederick was to say, "The princess is not ugly, but she is not beautiful...." — not exactly a ringing endorsement. Moreover, the prince's sisters found their new sister-in-law "unattractive and malodorous"... and they said so.

Frederick openly expressed his unsympathetic views on "political marriages built on nothing that bound two human beings together."

In the case of Elisabeth, I was not physically attracted to her. But out of respect and empathy for her plight having been forced to marry the likes of me, who cared for her naught, I set her up in a distant wing of the palace when she needed to be onsite, and in her own palace miles away where she could live on her own. I recall doing this so she could have privacy. So she could live her private life in whatever way she chose.

My definition of devotion was not blind obedience to the principle we today call "faithfulness." It was respecting the other's wishes.

Especially in a time where marriages were arranged for political reasons that often affected the daily lives of millions of other people in each of the betrothed's nations, I felt that marriage was a farce. It was just a tool for greater national ends. So, rightly or wrongly, I treated it that way.

But, being saddled with it as a cultural norm, I made the best of it on a practical level. I did my best to demonstrate respect for the woman in my formal relationship, the Queen, by providing her with and honoring her privacy accordingly. Moreover, giving her that privacy also meant it included her engagements with her lovers…that same privacy in the palace I gave myself with the women whom I engaged with over the years.

Love of Sex

As I recall with Marcus and Richard, Frederick was a lover of sex, but not controlled by the desire itself. Frederick is quoted as having said in French that he loved sex and that he was not cut out to be a monogamous husband.

The Crown Prince lost his virginity when he was first seduced at 16 by an older much more "experienced" woman of 21, the Countess Anna Orzelska, the daughter of Augustus II of Poland, having caught her eye at a month-long party hosted by her father at his court for all the dignitaries of Europe. Augustus II was a tall man for the times at 5'9" with bear-like physical strength, breaking horseshoes with his bare hands, and allegedly fathering more than 350 illegitimate children and one legitimate child. The court of "August the Strong" had the worst reputation in Europe, and he openly encouraged his daughter the Countess's scandalous behavior of smoking, drinking and having multiple affairs.

At the party, Augustus saw the young prince making eyes at his daughter, and to discourage him (some contemporaries surmised jealousy as a basis), Augustus offered Frederick a painting of a nude woman lying in a bed if he agreed to abandon his pursuit of the Countess. The prince agreed, later displaying the painting prominently in his palace.

However, shortly thereafter, the Countess secretly found her way to Berlin and to the prince's bedroom. So, in the end, Frederick enjoyed the company of both ladies, the one in the painting and the one for whom the painting was given. He dedicated poetry and musical works of his own composition to the one who introduced him as a teenager to the pleasures of sex.

There are also accounts in the book of letters I have that reference one of Frederick's senior counsel describing how he "regularly ferried women in and out of the royal chambers" during the king's adult years. The King had many female friends, and "loved the company and correspondence of charming women."

He also bought paintings of five pairs of nude lovers and hung them in his concert room. He found out they had come from the Holy Roman Emperor's apartments in Vienna where the Emperor's mother Maria Theresa (also the mother of Marie Antoinette, later Queen of France) had put them on the market thinking they were too erotic.

They depicted Diana and Endymion, Acis and Galatea, Bacchus and Ariadne, Zephys and Flora, and Venus and Adonis — all lovers from Greek myths. The back story of who previously owned them and why they were available so amused Frederick that he had to buy them. While I do not have direct recollection of this story, I am sure I found it hysterical at the time. Consequently, "Frederick put them on very public display in his concert room which was frequented by friends and dignitaries from across Europe."

I am certain that he was further entertained by the fact that he had already been in two wars pitted against Maria Theresa in her role as ruler of Austria and other lands, defeating her in both instances. This purchase was yet another way to "socially defeat" her, without her knowledge, by letting his guests know the prior ownership history of these paintings. Quite the proverbial "win-win" for Frederick over one of his arch rivals.

However, even though he loved sex, Frederick — much like I recall about Marcus and Richard — also had a preference for sometimes being alone. He enjoyed thinking, ruminating on ideas and concepts. Unlike most men, sex was not a driver for him. Like Richard the Lionheart and Marcus Aurelius, it did not "rule" his psychology, nor his body or behavior.

All of these men shared the self-perception and inner experience that they were comfortable both within themselves, and thus being by themselves. And in fact, all of them needed their "alone time" to reflect and rejuvenate from time to time. All were deep thinkers, and that required a certain degree of mental, emotional, physical and psychic energy to function at the level at which they each lived their respective lives.

Calmness Amidst Chaos

The following experience is reminiscent of many memories I have of dodging cannonballs during battles while riding and directing troops on horseback. Although I do not recall this story specifically, it is illustrative of Frederick's calmness in battle that I do recall similarly experiencing very clearly from my life as Richard the Lionheart.

Frederick had the uncanny ability to remain calm while cannonballs were literally exploding around him.

In June 1734, his father gave him his first battlefield command when Frederick, then colonel of a regiment, was just 22 years old. The young prince led 10,000 Prussians, who joined forces against the French, with the Imperial Army led by Prince François Eugène de Savoie Carignan, better known as "Prince Eugen." Prince Eugen was a field marshal in the army of the Holy Roman Empire. Frederick's father had written a message to the 71-year old Eugen that the Crown Prince delivered to him, imploring the experienced and great military commander to teach his son all he knew. The two got along well, and the general was very forthcoming with his battlefield knowledge, advising the young prince to, "Read military history. And always keep the great objectives of a campaign in view." Frederick, never shy and always forward looking, openly gave Eugen his own views on the condition of Europe. They talked about the art of war and the present situation before them.

One day, Frederick was allowed to ride out with a reconnaissance party to the battlefield to observe the French positions, when suddenly they were fired on by experienced French artillery specifically directed at Frederick. Suddenly, the cannon fire caused the Prussian troops around him to break ranks and begin to run.

Frederick calmly said, "Please excuse me, sir," to the general, and galloped off beelining it into the fray, straight into the heart of the battle to rally his Prussian troops. His fellow officers — not to mention the general — were both horrified and terrified, fearing for Frederick's life, as the enemy's cannonballs exploded all around him.

He successfully rallied his troops, got them reorganized back in the fight, and soon rejoined the general. Back alongside Eugen, Frederick calmly said, "I'm sorry we were interrupted... what I was about to say, General, was...." And he smoothly continued where they had left off earlier in their conversation, as if nothing had happened in the interim.

After this incident, Eugen reportedly told Frederick's father, "He will not only make a good soldier, but a great general."

Chapter 23

Personality

Marcus Aurelius and Frederick the Great

Now, let's delve a little deeper into their respective personalities — especially Frederick's since we have already described Marcus in detail earlier — and see how similar their traits may have been with each other. Are there perhaps sufficient connections of the "dots of data" between these two men's personalities to draw any further meaningful inferences?

Intellectuals of Their Times

As is well-known, the 2nd century Roman emperor Marcus Aurelius wrote what later turned out to be volumes of maxims that he intended as self-reflections to guide him in his own life from day to day. Some of them were first mentioned in 350 A.D. by a pagan philosopher Themistius, then they went unmentioned until around 900 A.D. when they were referenced by the Suda, a large 10th century Byzantine encyclopedia. They were finally collected and put into a printed version in 1559, the Gutenberg printing press having been invented in the 1450's.

So, by the time of Frederick the Great in the 1700's, not only were Marcus's "Meditations" well known, but also who he was as a philosopher-king was widely recognized throughout Europe.

Similarly, Frederick is known for having written his famous 1739 essay the *Anti-Machiavel* which attacked Machiavelli for his advocacy of what Frederick viewed as abusive and manipulative political leadership policies promoted in the 16th century book, *The Prince*. In Frederick's essay, he launches a chapter-by-chapter rebuttal of the principles propounded in *The Prince*. He said, "it is the duty of government to inspire princes to lead with the goal of happiness, prosperity and liberty of the people."

Frederick wrote this at age 27. While its authorship was an open secret, the essay, written in French, soon became widely read which catapulted Frederick's reputation throughout European intellectual circles. It was published in September 1740, a few months after his coronation at age 28.

Essentially, Frederick argues for a rational and benevolent ideal of statesmanship — that a king or leader is charged with the health and prosperity of their people. Interestingly, some historians have seen in Frederick's writing of this essay a mode of expression reminiscent of Marcus Aurelius's *Meditations*. The British historical biographer Frank McLynn goes even further to say that Frederick's work the *Anti-Machiavel* was intended to be written using Marcus's idiom. Perhaps it is not merely the mode of expression of their words, but also reflective of an expression of the minds or personalities of these all too similar men.

Students of Roman and Greek Philosophy

Both Frederick and Marcus were avid students of Roman and Greek philosophy. They shared a deep interest in Stoic philosophy in particular.

Marcus was educated by then famous, hand-selected philosophy tutors throughout his childhood. By far the greatest influence of all his tutors was the Stoic philosopher, Quintus Junius Rusticus.

Rusticus taught Marcus that to live the life of a philosopher was not a matter of showy austerity — wearing hair shirts, sleeping on the floor, wearing philosopher's cloaks, and other external trappings. It was "simply knowing how to live well." *That* was living the life of a philosopher. By viewing a philosopher through that lens, Rusticus argued that anyone could be one — whether he be a shepherd or an emperor.

Like all Stoics, Rusticus stressed "simplicity of style, and lucidity as against verbal fireworks." It was Rusticus who introduced Marcus to the discourses of Epictetus, the famous Greek Stoic philosopher who taught that philosophy is a way of life and not simply a theoretical discipline. To Epictetus, "all external events are beyond our control, and we should accept whatever happens calmly and dispassionately. However, individuals are responsible for their own actions, which they can examine and control through rigorous self-discipline."

Frederick often quoted Stoic and Epicurean ideals. Furthermore, he loved to study the ideas of the Greek philosophers Plato and Socrates.

At age 24 when Frederick was still a young prince, his father gave him the palace of Rheinsberg, which would become the Crown Prince's private retreat for the next four years. It was a small baroque *schloss*, or palace, on a lake with an amphitheater of oak woods. He wrote his first books there, and continued to amass his library in one of the towers. Since he had started collecting books at age 14, by the time he was at Rheinsberg ten years later, the collection already had grown to over 4,000 volumes.

Frederick also convened a small group of eleven close friends who met there regularly to discuss a wide range of topics, including philosophy, music and the art of war. The twelve of them called themselves "The Bayard Order," and each member had a distinct, unique pseudonym used at their get togethers.

Moreover, instead of calling this palace by its publicly known name, Rheinsberg, Frederick instead renamed it "Remusberg" for their special group's meetings. When I learned of that renaming, I immediately recalled why.

This was Frederick's personal "shout out" honoring Remus, the slain brother from the ancient legend of the naming of Rome. As the story goes, in 753 B.C. Remus was killed by his brother (and fellow demigod) Romulus in a fraternal feud over who would rule the city. And thus, Rome was named after the victorious brother.

As a lifelong student of Roman history, Frederick knew this legend verbatim. By naming his palace Remusberg, the Prussian king was honoring the slain brother, Remus.

Perhaps Frederick felt like he was "balancing the historical legend," that the story of fratricide should not be praised, and that it should not endure, at least not unfettered. And maybe Frederick felt like he was doing his small part to "right that wrong" by naming his palace in honor of Remus.

Whatever the actual reason, Frederick clearly wanted to cement that honor in at least the minds of his close group of eleven friends who gathered regularly to discuss, among other things, ancient Rome as well as Greek philosophy — Stoicism in particular. So, he had them call his palace by its "new" name, Remusberg.

Were all these overlaps in Frederick and Marcus's interests in ancient Rome and Greek philosophy a coincidence? Or were they perhaps based on something inherent and deeper within? And was there an ancient connection with the number twelve in reference to how many members there were in this small group of close friends, the Bayard Order?

Food for thought.

Mutual Connection With Antoninus Pius

It is also interesting and noteworthy that Frederick explicitly stated that he "modeled his life after Marcus Aurelius."

Moreover, as we mentioned earlier in our book, Frederick sought out and purchased a Roman statue of superb quality that was sculpted in the 2nd century during the reign of the Roman emperor Antoninus Pius, and placed it prominently in the garden at his favorite Prussian palace, *Sanssouci*. Here is a little more background.

Who was Antoninus Pius? He was Marcus Aurelius's stepfather who immediately preceded him as emperor of Rome.

Marcus was still a teenager when Antoninus "ascended to the purple" upon Hadrian's death. Marcus learned a lot from observing and shadowing his stepfather in his role as emperor. Moreover, Antoninus situated Marcus in senior leadership roles in the Roman Senate at the young ages of 17, 19 and 22, as quaestor and twice as consul, to get the senatorial leadership used to seeing Marcus as a leader and to help train Marcus through taking on those positions. Antoninus even changed the law, temporarily revoking the minimum age requirement of

After the Afterlife

24, so that Marcus could serve in these positions. Afterwards, Antoninus changed the law back to 24.

When Antoninus designated the 19-year old Marcus as his co-consul in 140 A.D., he gave Marcus the title of "Caesar." In his second round as consul at 22 years old, Marcus received the unprecedented privilege of being able to introduce five different pieces of legislation in the Senate — the most any emperor was even allowed. Soon thereafter, coins showing Marcus as Caesar were struck. This all occurred while Antoninus was Emperor of Rome. Marcus would not yet become emperor for another seventeen years.

Consequently, Marcus, as he also wrote in what are today known as his *Meditations*, was vocal in expressing his gratitude, respect and love for his stepfather Antoninus. Significantly, Marcus did not write those maxims thinking they would ever become public knowledge, further underscoring that he was truly expressing his candid, honest feelings about Antoninus in them.

On some level, whether conscious or subconscious, could Frederick have acted out of that deep and ancient love for Antoninus by buying that 1600-year old Roman sculpture and prominently displaying it in his palace garden?

Dislike For Regal Status

Another similarity between Frederick and Marcus is that neither man wanted the regal role. Frederick wanted to be a poet and Marcus a philosopher. They each would have much preferred to have been "regular guys." And their recorded behavior in terms of how they treated others reflected that. Neither man ever exhibited any fondness for the status or pomp of their positions as leaders of large empires. They each saw their roles as holders of the responsibility for the lives and well-being of their people. And they both acted in their roles accordingly, never acting out of personal gain, always acting in what they felt were the best interests of the citizenry they ruled.

Notwithstanding their distaste for taking on the regal positions in their respective cultures, both men rose to the occasion and ruled responsibly, viewing themselves as "trustees in the service of their people." I find this commonality in leadership style quite remarkable, especially given that these men lived in completely different cultures in different parts of Europe — 1600 years apart.

Chapter 24

Personality

Sitting Bull

1831-1890

Thoughtful, Careful, Deliberate

I remember being slow and careful from birth. I espoused and practiced the "think before you act" maxim. No one had taught that to me yet, I just knew it in my core. There are many stories recorded by the contemporary journalists who interviewed those who observed Sitting Bull from when he was a youth through his adulthood.

Interestingly, much like Richard and Frederick, when Sitting Bull was an infant, the adults around him remarked on his habit of being careful and deliberate.

Historians have recorded that the young boy, who would later become Chief of the Hunkpapa Lakota and much later the supreme chief of all the autonomous bands or tribes of the Lakota, at birth was first named Jumping Badger, then nicknamed *Hunkesni* ("Slow"), because as a toddler, he was more careful and deliberate than most children his age — unhurried and thus, "slow." Instead of grabbing randomly at things, he handled them and examined them carefully.

As a slightly older child, he "rarely rushed into trouble or made unwise decisions." In the opinions expressed by contemporary adult observers, this particular behavior of the child "paid respect to his intelligence."

The following story reflects that wisdom especially at such a young age around seven or eight years old:

A chirping bird woke the young boy from a nap, warning him to lie perfectly still, while a grizzly bear passed "so close that he could feel the damp warmth of its fetid breath." From that moment on, the yellow-shafted flicker held a special place in his heart because that bird had saved his life.

Later at 14, his father changed his son's name to "Tatanka-Iyotanka" — Sitting Bull. The actual meaning of Sitting Bull is "the bison bull who resides among us," i.e., a strong and wise being had come to "sit" or live among the Lakota.

A Shaman

Sitting Bull was a *wichasa wakan*, i.e., a seer, a holy man with an inborn ability to understand the past and see into the future through dreams and visions. He was a member of several dream societies, groups of men from the seven different Lakota tribes in the Dakotas who would share their dream experiences, including insights and predictions of the future.

My initial memories of that lifetime as a shaman confused me because I also had visions of myself leading meetings of senior leaders in that same lifetime. I seemed to be acting as the head of those meetings. And I didn't know of any shamans, or "medicine men," who were leading tribes. When I first started having these memories, I had assumed it was an "either/or" proposition.

Many decades later, when I had the experience in my Austin living room where I identified myself as Sitting Bull, I read that he had also been a shaman who had had psychic experiences. I also learned that when Sitting Bull was in his mother's womb, he heard and recalled what was said. And later after he was born, he recounted this accurately to his mother and others who had been present while he was *in utero*.

He once told a newspaper reporter in 1877: "I am a free man. I see. I know. I began to see when I was not yet born, when I was not in my mother's arms, but inside my mother's belly. It was there that I began to study about my people...[The Great Spirit]...gave me the power to see out of the womb. I studied there, in the womb, about many things... I was so interested that I turned over on my side. The Great Spirit must have told me at that time...that I would be the man to be the judge of all the other Indians — a big man to decide for them in all their ways."

When I read this, I recalled being frustrated as a young newborn infant child with not being able to do and express yet in words — at least that could be understood by others — everything I was thinking.

Predicting the Outcome of the Battle of Little Bighorn

I do not explicitly recall this experience of predicting the outcome of that battle, although the experience of being a shaman and having shamanistic experiences — visions and predictive dreams — is something that I have recalled from this 19th century lifetime for many decades now.

According to reports by Lakota contemporaries of Sitting Bull, just weeks before the now famous battle with Custer's troops, Sitting Bull predicted the outcome in a dream — that Custer would lose the battle, and he and all his men would die.

It was in the camp at Little Bighorn River that Sitting Bull, then a revered leader and holy man, participated in the *Wiwang Wacipi*, the Sun Dance ceremony, where he danced for 36 hours in a row in front of the sacred tree, making 50 sacrificial cuts on each arm before falling into a trance. Normally the cuts would be made in his chest and back, however he already bore too many scars there from previous Sun Dances. His high pain threshold is reminiscent of what I experienced after my foot was cut by a tomahawk at the Boy Scout camp when I was a teenager in this current lifetime.

When he awoke from his trance, Sitting Bull revealed that he had a vision of U.S. soldiers "falling like grasshoppers from the sky," which he interpreted as an omen that the U.S. Army would soon be defeated. Sitting Bull told everyone, "Hundreds of bluecoats would attack us, but we would destroy them."

On June 25, 1876, Lieutenant Colonel George Armstrong Custer's cavalry tried to attack the huge encampment of 7,000 Lakota from the north at the opposite end of the Little Bighorn River. This was probably the largest encampment of Plains Indians ever assembled, which had over 15,000 horses alone. However, the Lakota-Cheyenne alliance of over 3,000 warriors — armed with 200 repeating Henry rifles (able to fire three times faster than Custer's single-shot Springfield carbines), as well as bows and arrows, knives and tomahawks — easily triumphed in the Battle of the Little Bighorn, overwhelming Custer's smaller force of 210 troopers. Custer and every single one of his men were killed when most of them scattered, dying in the gullies and ravines — while a handful, including Custer, retreated and clustered at the top of a small hill where they hardly fired a single shot before being overrun. Only about 100 native people lost their lives. The entire battle lasted less than one hour.

True to Sitting Bull's prophetic dream, the "blue coats" — the U.S. cavalry led by George Armstrong Custer — were unequivocally defeated in that battle. Sitting Bull told his braves not to mutilate the corpses of the troopers, but in their excitement, drunk with the overwhelming victory, the braves could not restrain themselves. The scalping and dismemberment of many of the troopers was rampant, as the braves believed that doing so would impede the dead's transition into their afterlife. Sitting Bull knew this would be a mistake with severe repercussions.

In the victory celebration that evening at the new encampment we had moved to, some asked me if that battle was the fulfillment of my vision during the Sun Dance. "Regretfully," I said, "an even greater assault is yet to come."

I knew that the U.S. government would not stop now at destroying us. They had already reneged on their agreements to supply us with sufficient food rations, instead trying to starve us to death while they had us confined to the reservations. That's why my friend Chief Gall and many other frustrated Lakota had left the reservation and joined us, all convening at the Little Bighorn River, so we could find food to eat — for our very survival. Pushed to the brink, we had been quite ready to stand and fight the *wasichus* ("white men") when Custer and his men launched their surprise attack.

But I knew what would happen next. We had humiliated them in that battle and they would make Custer a martyr. I had seen that game played out before in my previous lifetimes.

Piercing Eyes and Sense of Humor

As with Richard the Lionheart, Sitting Bull was a man with a great sense of humor. "His brown eyes had the mischievous twinkle of one who enjoyed a hearty laugh. When he stared at someone, his eyes seemed to stab into that person's soul, reading his or her deepest thoughts."

Such were the words of one of the many English speaking writers reporting about Sitting Bull, especially after Custer's deathly debacle at the Little Bighorn became "front-page" national news. Now, every journalist wanted to interview him, because the public was eager to know more about this chief. Who was the leader of these people who were determined to stand in the way of American expansion? "How dare he...," was the American public sentiment.

Descriptions of this Lakota chief and shaman, Sitting Bull, began to flood the newsstands across America. Reporters used the word "Sioux" — instead of Lakota — to describe this tribe of people, not realizing that Sioux is a derogative term never used by the Lakota about themselves.

"Sioux" is actually a disparaging term meaning "snake" used by the rival Ojibwa tribe for the Dakota and Lakota people. But when European explorers first asked the Ojibwa what the neighboring tribe was called, it went down in history as the Sioux.

Notwithstanding the depressing dilemma that Sitting Bull found thrust upon himself and his people, over which he had little or no control, he nevertheless found a way to bring a note of wryness and even humor into situations whenever possible.

A story about Sitting Bull stands out that illustrates this element of his personality. The man was an enigma at best — an interesting mix of what some might view as contrasting traits. He was not impulsive, nor was he unemotional. And he was said to be "gifted with the power of sarcasm…."

One cold winter afternoon in the early 1880's after he had succumbed to the efforts by the U.S. government to confine and isolate him and his people onto reservations, he was sitting on a bench in front of his cabin with his two wives on the Standing Rock Sioux Reservation, which straddles the border of both South and North Dakota. In the distance, he saw an approaching buckboard easily identified by the cloud of dust surrounding it, stirred up by the wagon wheels.

Sitting Bull knew exactly who was driving the wagon and the question he would be asked, when it finally reached his door. Sure enough, as the wagon got closer he and his wives could see that it was the minister from the local church.

The minister climbed down from the buckboard and approached Sitting Bull, shaking the dust from his black hat. The minister exchanged a few pleasantries and then got right to the point admonishing the great Lakota leader, "It is un-Christian of you to have two wives. It is against the will of God. And it is barbarian and heathen."

Sitting Bull sat there with his head cocked and listened patiently to the outburst of the minister, letting this self-pro-claimed "man of God" vent. Finally, Sitting Bull raised his hand to quiet the angry minister and waved his hand at his two wives and said to him, "Well, there they are — *you* tell them which one has to leave."

Not only did it display Sitting Bull's sense of humor — although the minister certainly did not find it funny — but perhaps even more importantly, it also showed the pure Lakota logic of why their tradition and custom of taking care of women existed.

Which of these Lakota women would be deprived of a loving home? In our native culture, it was felt that no woman should have to fend for herself, that every woman should be allowed to bear children, and that she and her children deserved to be cared for, sheltered and protected. I felt it was barbaric to do otherwise.

So, I say, who is "the barbarian and the heathen" in that picture? The one who leaves women and children to protect and fend for themselves on the streets of America? Or the one who nurtures and cares for them if no one else will help them?

Confident and At Peace

Much like when I was Richard and Frederick, I knew at an early age my role was to lead. I was not particularly fond of the idea when I was Frederick, but by the time I was Sitting Bull, I was more in touch with my inner world, and I was at peace with my responsibilities.

Historians also record that Sitting Bull "radiated self-confidence," and was a man "at peace within himself." He stood 5'9", 175 pounds, and was a strong man, both mentally and physically — inside and out. By comparison, the average size of the U.S. cavalryman at Little Bighorn was 5'7", 150 pounds.

From birth, Sitting Bull had a sense of destiny, knew who he was, and his reason for being. As he told everyone after his birth, he knew when he was in his mother's womb that he would be a leader of his nation.

Ethical and Empathetic

I remember treating my word as my ethical duty to uphold. If I said I would tend to the horses, I did it as if the Great Spirit had told me to. I viewed my promise as my bond to myself and the world. I did not take it lightly. And in my heart, I was a pacifist. I only fought because I had to. Many lifetimes before this one, I had grown tired of fighting. I only killed animals for food and sustenance. I did it out of need. Not out of enjoyment.

The historians also record that Sitting Bull had strict moral principles. The violence of the warpath ended when he returned home to the village and his family. He lived peacefully, honoring his obligations as head of household taking care of his wives and children.

He was "a loyal friend, never broke a promise or deceived anyone." He was a "kind and gentle man, and the sight of a sick child filled his eyes with tears." My connection with children continues in my present lifetime. They "see" me and I "see" them.

Wooden Leg, a warrior who fought beside Sitting Bull, said it best: "He had a kind heart and good judgment as to the best course of conduct. He was strong in religion — the Indian religion. He had a big brain and a good one, a strong heart and a generous one."

Protector of Women and Children

To this day, if I hear of abuse or mistreatment of women or children, I get incensed. I have had this response as long as I can remember in this current lifetime. Until I had these memories of similar reactions in my lifetimes as Marcus, Richard and Sitting Bull, I did not realize where this "old" trait had come from.

I find that type of behavior unacceptable and reprehensible — regardless of whether the abuser seeks excuse or justification based on religious, cultural or the alleged educational reason to deliver "punishment where deserved to teach a lesson." There is no good reason for the subjugation or mistreatment of anyone — man, woman or child. I feel in my core that the mistreatment of those, who by no fault of their own are physically weaker, is inexcusable. Instead, it is a sign of profound weakness of the abuser or abusing groups. I still am moved by a deep visceral reaction when I hear of such transgressions, especially by men upon women and children.

According to the well-known physician and writer, Charles A. Eastman, who interviewed Sitting Bull as well as many of his contemporaries for many decades after the great chief was killed, Sitting Bull never killed any women or children. Moreover, Sitting Bull never attacked a white settlement, and was known to have freed white women and children captives.

In fact, there was one instance where a group of white men had attacked, raped and killed an entire Lakota village's population of women and children. Subsequently, in a retaliatory battle led by Sitting Bull, the Lakota had captured a group of the attackers' women and children. Consequently, the Lakota leaders wanted to allow their warriors to deliver the same measure as punishment on those women and children as their loved ones had experienced.

Sitting Bull would not allow it.

He had those white women and children safely escorted back to the nearest U.S. Army fort. I distinctly recall seeing visions of returning white women and their children to the "blue coats" fort. I remember this outraged my fellow Lakota leaders, but because I was immoveable in this decision and was their senior leader, they had to acquiesce.

One of my distinct, detailed memories is remembering saying, in Lakota, to those other Lakota leaders: "We do not act like the white man. They are the savages, not us. We know what is right. What they did was wrong. We are not animals like they are. It is wrong to kill women and children. Women and children do not deserve to be killed for the bad behavior of their men."

Another incident reported to contemporary journalists involved a young boy who was taken captive in a battle with the Assiniboine tribe. Sitting Bull would not allow his warriors to kill the boy. The chief saved his life. He adopted the boy as his brother. "Hohay," as the boy was called, became devoted to Sitting Bull and was responsible in his later years, by sharing stories with reporters, in helping the Lakota chief gain even greater fame.

Pragmatism

I recall always having a pragmatic view of the world. There are reports by historians that, when asked about allowing the non-Lakota doctors to treat our sick using *wasichu* ("white man") medical solutions, Sitting Bull's response was practical: "The main thing is to cure the patient — any method that works is a good one."

I remember being a believer in my Lakota people's religion of praying to the Great Spirit, and I have specific recollections as a shaman of performing ceremonies and rites in that tradition. Much later when we were being confined to reservations by the U.S. government, they sent Christian missionaries to try to convert us to their religion. I reportedly once asked a missionary, "What does it matter how I pray, so long as my prayers are answered?" Again, this was a window into my pragmatic view of the world, even from a religious standpoint.

Negotiation Skills

As I recall with Marcus, Richard and Frederick, Sitting Bull was skilled in negotiating. I remember negotiating many deals. Some were with the other tribes, some were within my own Lakota tribe, and still others were attempts to negotiate with the U.S. government, after we realized that we could not outfight them.

Historians also have recorded that Sitting Bull was a born diplomat and in his middle and later years, he spent less time on the warpath and more time as counselor for his people. He had become the supreme chief of all of the Lakota tribes in 1867. During that time he retained his status as a war chief, however he was not supposed to actually take part in fights anymore. Instead, he was supposed to take on the role of peacemaker.

In October 1888, he traveled to Washington, DC along with sixty other chiefs to meet with U.S. government officials from the Indian Bureau within the Interior Department, who were hoping to negotiate and get an agreement signed with the Lakota regarding compensation for their lands.

Soon after the Lakota chief's arrival in Washington, at 237 Pennsylvania Avenue above a cigar store, Sitting Bull gave a two-hour speech that was followed closely by many in the country who read about it in their local media. According to the *Washington Post*: "Sitting Bull made the opening speech, and every word of it was closely listened to by the hearers. He spoke nearly 2 hours. His style is, even to a person who cannot understand him, very impressive, and his gestures though lavish, are graceful. He wags his head as he talks in a solemn way, and his remarks often elicited approving grunts from his companions. Sitting Bull favors accepting the terms of the Government with an amendment so as to increase the price of the land relinquished to the price paid by the settlers."

The government's initial offer was $.50 per acre. Sitting Bull convinced John Grass, an Indian who had been co-opted to change his name, to negotiate it up to $1.25 per acre. The government came back with a counteroffer of $1.00 per acre. Sitting Bull met with his delegation and led the opposition to the plan proposing that they dig in their heels at $1.25 per acre and insist on an immediate cash payment rather than having the money paid out over five or more years. The government rejected it, and Sitting Bull and his fellow chiefs returned to the reservation in the Dakotas without a deal.

Sitting Bull was already well aware of the government's duplicity and bad faith dealing, having already experienced their reneging on other treaties between the parties. He left Washington disappointed but not surprised.

I learned the hard way that in any negotiation when one party is at the table in bad faith, no real agreement can be reached. Moreover, if any so-called agreement is reached, it cannot be trusted.

Charming the *Wasichu* Ladies

I resurfaced parts of this following memory about Sitting Bull's visit to Washington, DC to negotiate on behalf of the Lakota and other nations. I had a recollection of being with a large group of *wasichu* women (white women) all dressed up in their — what appeared to me at the time anyway — formal dresses. However, at that moment, I did not know why I was with them in the nation's capital. I just "saw" myself surrounded by them sitting in a living room setting.

Later, I read this account of an event during that trip that took place in the Belvedere House, where Sitting Bull "held court in the parlor above the rear of the hotel lobby."

The *Washington Post* reporter covering the gathering noted that, "The ladies of the hotel seemed very much taken with the

Indian warrior. They shook hands with him and gazed fondly into his classic face, while he in turn, told a lady that she looked like Mrs. Sitting Bull, only her hair wasn't red, and he asked for a lock of her hair." The lady reportedly laughed. Other accounts reported how charming Sitting Bull was with the ladies.

Crow Foot, 1876-1890

I remember who Sitting Bull's favorite son Crow Foot is today. The more I uncovered about Crow Foot's personality, the clearer it became to me.

Crow Foot was born just before the Battle of the Little Bighorn in the same year. He was named in honor of "Crow Foot" — the great chief of the Blackfeet in Canada with whom Sitting Bull had just smoked the peace pipe. Sitting Bull's obituary recalls the young boy Crow Foot as "bright as a dollar with eyes that fairly snap like whips."

Sitting Bull believed that his children needed to learn to read and write, so he placed all of them in the local school run by the Christian missionaries (Congregational Day School). Crow Foot was said by his teachers to be "strong and healthy," "a solemn youth," who "displayed a wisdom remarkable for one so young."

According to a contemporary biographer Robert P. Higheagle (whose father was present at Sitting Bull's death), "Crow Foot was not like the rest of the boys. He did not get out and mingle with the boys and play their games. He grew old too early." Crow Foot "took his heritage seriously and even in his adolescence began to give advice to his father on weighty matters."

Sitting Bull surrendered to the U.S. government on July 20, 1881 at Fort Buford in present-day North Dakota. At Fort Buford, the beleaguered Lakota chief handed his 1866 Winchester rifle to Crow Foot to then give to the government officer, Major Brotherton. I think by doing so, Sitting Bull was symbolically connecting his five-year old son to the act of his agreeing to surrender. Accordingly, he explicitly told the government officer that he wanted them to educate his son so that he could thrive in this new world of the "white man," that the defeated chief saw as an inevitability for Crow Foot's generation.

According to historical records, in Sitting Bull's own words: "I surrender this rifle to you through my young son, whom I now desire to teach in this manner that he has become a friend of the Americans. I wish him to learn the habits of the whites and to be educated as their sons are educated. I wish it to be remembered that I was the last man of my tribe to surrender my rifle. This boy has given it to you, and he now wants to know how he is going to make a living."

Sitting Bull's words reflect his hope that the U.S. government would finally honor its commitments to the Lakota and other Natives. His hope unfortunately never manifested, and near the end of his life, Sitting Bull finally was forced to accept that the government was incapable of honoring its promises.

To this day that remains a regret that I have carried for over 130 years — the sorrow that I was not able to protect my people from the self-serving greed of the U.S. government and its supporters. Emotionally for me it has been the most difficult burden to let go of — my inability to move them sufficiently off of their "we must have it all" viewpoint towards a middle ground where we could all live together peacefully in a place of mutual co-existence.

I still wrestle with the reality of accepting that their position, founded in their belief in "Manifest Destiny," eventually led to the cultural destruction and genocide of my Plains people and our fellow brothers and sisters of other nations (tribes) throughout North America in the 1800's. Perhaps even more strongly today because I have had 130 years to contemplate their belief in Manifest Destiny, I reject that belief: that the United States was "destined" by their "God" to expand across our Great Plains to the Pacific Ocean killing all in its path. What so-called "God" would mandate that? No god or great spirit that my people would ever pray to — then or today.

Sitting Bull's Death

This story reveals another key characteristic of Crow Foot's personality.

According to the official government reports, in the early morning hours of December 15, 1890, with an icy drizzle filling the air, a group of Lakota, who had been deputized as police officers by Chief of Police Bullhead, approached Sitting Bull's camp to arrest him. They chose early morning before sunrise to not only surprise Sitting Bull preventing him from escaping, but also to minimize stirring his followers who were still asleep.

Several of the policemen entered Sitting Bull's cabin, leaving the rest of the armed force outside the house. They woke up the chief who was sleeping in bed with one of his wives, naked as was his habit…even in the winter.

After taking possession of his two rifles and allowing him to dress, the police pushed Sitting Bull out of his cabin. Eyewitnesses say the special police brought him out about 30 yards surrounding him with a cordon of about 30-40 policemen, and paused.

Standing at the cabin door, Sitting Bull's 14-year old son Crow Foot cried out, chiding his father, "You have always called yourself a brave chief. Now you are allowing yourself to be taken by the *ceska maza* (police)."

Crow Foot's impassioned words triggered something deep within his father. For several moments, Sitting Bull was lost in thought.

Sitting Bull then declared in Lakota, "Then I shall not go."

Someone, from the large crowd that had gathered, shouted, "You shall not take away our chief!"

A shot rang out and Bullhead fell forward mortally wounded, and as he fell, fired a shot which entered Sitting Bull's chest, shattering his spine. Then Red Tomahawk shot Sitting Bull again, in the back of the head. Chief Sitting Bull was killed instantly.

Crow Foot was also shot and killed.

As was reported by Robert P. Higheagle after speaking to an eyewitness, "My relative Lone Man told me that it was Crow Foot who urged his father Sitting Bull to resist the Indian policemen the day the chief was killed. It was like Crow Foot to do that."

What was also striking about these events was that they caused me to "recognize" the emotional, verbal and behavioral tendencies of my current son Jesse, born in 1988, with my son Crow Foot, born in 1876 — and how similar they are to each other psycho-emotionally. As I then reviewed more closely examples of Crow Foot's personality traits described by his contemporaries, the recognition became even clearer. And then a few years ago I "connected the dots," and had this knowingness and recognition of seeing that it was my son again, together with me once more 98 years later.

Jesse is a quick-witted young man, who can have a tongue as sharp as his mind at times. While he loves his father, he is not afraid to call him out if he feels it necessary, as he did on that icy cold December morning in 1890. The depth of his wisdom belies his youthful age — he is a sage much older than his years. And I love him today as much as I did then when he was my favorite son.

Sitting Bull the Human Being

In his book, *Sitting Bull: The Life and Times of an American Patriot*, historical biographer Robert M. Utley states that he tried to view the Lakota chief from the white as well as the Indian perspective. According to Utley, Sitting Bull emerges from both perspectives "as an enduring legend and a historical icon, but above all as a truly great human being."

Sitting Bull the Old Friend

James M. Walsh had become very close friends with Sitting Bull, whom he called "Bull," when Walsh was the regional North-West Mounted Police Superintendent providing safe refuge to the 5,000 Lakota who fled north to Saskatchewan for several years after the Battle of the Little Bighorn. They had become such close friends that before Sitting Bull returned to the U.S. to surrender, he gave Walsh his cherished war bonnet (headdress). When Walsh read in the local Winnipeg newspaper on December 16, 1890 of his old friend's death, he wrote these thoughts on his company stationery:

"I am glad to learn that Bull is relieved of his miseries even if it took the bullet to do it. A man who wields such power as Bull once did, that of a King, over a wild spirited people cannot endure abject poverty slavery and beggary without suffering great mental pain, and death is a relief....Bull's confidence and belief in the Great Spirit was stronger than I ever saw in any other man. He trusted to him implicitly....History does not tell us that a greater Indian than Bull ever lived, he was the Mohammat of his people, the law and king maker of the Sioux."

Sitting Bull

Crow Foot, son of Sitting Bull

249

Chapter 25

What's the Point?

For me, the answer is quite simple. I choose to learn more about who I am.

That means whether it's through experiences I have in this lifetime in the 21st century or if it's through a memory that might resurface from a 12th century lifetime. It is all data for me to draw upon to learn more about who I am now and how I can improve my living of life in the continual present, which is the basis for my future.

This oft-cited maxim comes to mind:

"Know Thyself"

That has been my conscious choice for at least the past 6,000 years that I am aware of. During that journey, I have put all of my experiences, including ones about past lives, through the crucible of rationality, logic and good old-fashioned common sense, as much as possible. Along the way, I have overlaid on top of that mental process an attempt to look at the past life experiences and my interpretations of them using reliable evidence as a filtration device — starting with the common sense view and whenever possible adding the external third-party corroborative element as possible further verification of the veracity of the memories.

For now anyway, I have not come up with a better rational explanation for the apparent past life experiences I've shared here. So, I'm logically left with the interpretation that I may actually have been those personalities through time, and that my experiences seem to be related to past lives.

I know it may be difficult for some people to accept that, and as I've said, that is not why I've written this book. I am a teacher, not a preacher.

My objective is not to convince or to change people's beliefs, but instead to pose different perspectives to consider — to create lenses for each of us to look through, first and foremost myself. By creating these various lenses, I endeavor to filter my own experiences in a way that makes sense, informs and explains, and ultimately teaches. To teach myself is always my primary goal.

Still, I question everything. I do not blindly follow even my own ideas. I am not married to the conclusions I've come to about who or what I may have been in these past lives.

What is much more important to me is what those lives may have taught me about myself, and how that has helped (and continues to help) me live my life today — in the continual, ever-developing present.

And secondarily, these experiences and recognitions of my personality traits, that seem to transverse time and space for millennia, are factors that give me fairly reliable assurances that I will continue retaining my core identity from lifetime to lifetime. I think that is true for each of us.

Yes, it can change over time, and some of those traits may manifest more strongly in one lifetime compared to another lifetime. But the essential personality traits seem to continue for a very, very long time. That I find heartening, because it is something we can "hang our hat on," "point our finger at," that seems to bolster the claims that we have heard for millennia from many NDE'ers, mediums, and other spiritually-oriented people that our minds continue not only after we die, but also from lifetime to lifetime.

Moreover, can some of those unmet hopes, wishes and dreams — simply put, our "desires" — traverse time and space within the vehicles of our minds from lifetime to lifetime? Can they affect our choices in our future lifetimes?

Could, for example, my early death in my 20's during World War II affect my current lifetime as far as my attraction to certain women and fashion styles? Could my failure to protect my native people in the 1800's, especially the women and children, affect me emotionally — with a reaction that may seem excessive — when I hear of child or spousal abuse in a subsequent lifetime? Could my present-day suspicion and general dismissal of most authority figures be attributable to my having been naïve in my acceptance of religious and govern-mental institutions over multiple lifetimes?

I think they could be.

And once we see those tendencies in ourselves — whether they be positive, negative or neutral in their effects on our daily lives — can we perhaps take advantage of that knowledge to improve our state of happiness, our degree of inner contentment?

I think so.

At least, that has been my experience in harvesting these memories and self-knowings. They have helped me enormously in improving my degree of inner peace.

Those are the takeaways and perspectives I hope I have been able to convey. And in doing so, I hope they will help you — both in your understanding of life and in developing your own growing sense of inner peace — in your eternal journey, starting now in this lifetime and in those going forward.

Chapter 26

Afterword

The "Jigsaw Puzzle" Analogy

The following image of a jigsaw puzzle has helped me wrap my mind around this whole concept of past life memories. I have found it especially useful in visualizing for myself how these often disparate and random tidbits of memories have trickled into my conscious awareness over the decades.

Here is the analogy.

I think of it like a huge jigsaw puzzle — as if one lifetime is the equivalent of a 100,000,000-piece puzzle. I'm randomly picking a massive number, but you can pick any number that is really, really big.

In this 21st century lifetime with my kids, I've done 500-piece jigsaw puzzles, and even a 1,000-piece "mind bender" once or twice. Those are very difficult jigsaw puzzles because there are so many little pieces and, to make an already difficult situation even worse, from a distance so many of them look alike. But upon closer examination, I could see that they were not exactly the same shape. Moreover, even though two pieces might *physically* fit together perfectly, sometimes I'd notice that the *pictorial designs* did not match properly. When that would happen, I'd have to start that section of the puzzle all over from scratch.

The advantage of course with the store-bought jigsaw puzzle is that it has a box cover. So at least I know what the outcome should look like. At least I have a picture of the final product to match the colors and designs against.

Unfortunately, past life memories come with no "box cover." They come with no map, no GPS. It's like getting a GPS message that tells you to "Go here," but you have no idea where "here" is in the larger scheme of things.

To make it even more complex, when I had my first past life memory in 1977, I didn't even know it had to do with a past life. Consequently, I wasn't even initially asking where it possibly fit into my historical timeline. Timeline? History? I thought I just had a really bad dream, a nightmare.

Once I did start to realize past life memories were resurfacing, very often I would find myself initially unable to tell *which* life it was fitting into, never mind *where* in that particular life. So that is why the "jigsaw puzzle" analogy has worked so well for me all these years. It has helped me make a very confusing confluence of experiences a little less confusing.

I have pictured myself putting these jigsaw puzzles together — piece by piece — with no box cover picture to guide me. I'd just patiently wait and see if and when more pieces would resurface for me to add to the sometimes growing puzzle. At times my puzzles have stagnated for decades with no additional pieces, with some even today seemingly stuck with a very limited number of pieces.

Furthermore, when my past life memories started resurfacing back in the late 1970's, I had no idea if I was eventually going to have one, two or ten different jigsaw puzzles (lifetimes) to which I would be adding puzzle segments (resurfacing memories). As it turned out, I ended up having memories from many different lifetimes — sometimes from several lifetimes concurrently.

And...when this started happening to me, I didn't even believe in reincarnation or past lives. When I think back on that period in my life now, it was pretty crazy, confusing and energizing — all at the same time.

On top of all that, as if it wasn't already difficult enough, I quickly began to notice the pieces of the jigsaw puzzle did not come to me in any particular order or organized manner. Just like my memories of this current lifetime — they typically came to me in a random way, not chronologically, just almost seemingly at their own whim, whenever my conscious mind would allow one to "slip through the turnstile."

On reflection, I guess it was no different from the way I recalled memories from this lifetime. For example, I don't remember this 21st century lifetime of mine in sequential order every time I stop and reflect about my life. Sure, I suppose I could. I could direct my mind to think chronologically about my life as Kelvin Chin. But if I'm just free floating, it usually just comes in random spurts — a little from that period of my life, a little from that other period, etc.

And, to maybe state the obvious, I don't remember *everything* that happened in my life — every bite of food I've taken, how many steps I've walked to and from my car to the supermarket, or what I said to the cashier four months ago, never mind 40 years ago. Plus, random events that are more emotionally charged seem to pop up more readily in the forefront of my memory. But even that is not an absolute rule. It's not always emotional ones in the front of my mind...sometimes they're just mundane memories too. Nothing seemingly special.

It's all over the map.

So that's exactly how randomly and "all over the map" — literally and figuratively — my two dozen lifetimes of memories have surfaced in me, memories that stretch back 6,000 years. And they keep unfolding. I keep getting new pieces to add to the jigsaw puzzles, here and there, even now.

So that's the big picture. But what about on a more granular level — how did the jigsaw puzzle analogy help me explain to myself what was going on?

At first, analogously I would get two or three pieces that fit together. Then maybe I got another 10 pieces that would fit together...but then, oops, sometimes I'd realize they didn't fit together after all. In fact, they may have had nothing to do with the two or three pieces that I initially got. And later it might become apparent that those 10 pieces represented another, completely different segment of that same life.

But then what happened?

I'd eventually get another five pieces that fit together and I'd have enough indicators that they were from a different lifetime because there would be something — the sensibility or feeling of the time period perhaps — that was different. So I'd know it wasn't from that original one.

Then I started to develop a combination of using logic and process-of-elimination (e.g., certain clothing or ship construction only existed in a given time period in history, or a certain language that may surface was spoken by a certain tribe or region of people) along with a "sixth sense" of just what could be called a "knowingness" about how things fit together… or didn't. And by using that process, I started to learn how to fit together which pieces in which puzzle goes with this puzzle or that puzzle — with this lifetime or that lifetime. Essentially I taught myself this process through trial and error.

After a year or two of my memories resurfacing, I began realizing I was developing sometimes as many as three to five to 10 puzzles going on at the same time. In other words, I would get 10 pieces in this puzzle and then a week or two, or maybe even two months or two years would go by — it would vary, there was no regularity to the timing at all — and I might get another 20 pieces in any of those other puzzles.

It was almost like my mind or consciousness was subconsciously "mining for memories" — and I would never know if I would "strike gold" or not. This was all spontaneous as I have mentioned. I was not "doing any exercises" or techniques to bring up these memories. And, as I mentioned, I have never had a past life regression with anyone. I was just living my "normal, everyday" life as a corporate or law firm executive, and these memories would surface all on their own.

But every once in a while, my mind would seem to hit a motherlode — as if I had hit this vein of precious gemstones like in mining. And when that serendipitous event would happen, I'd ride it. I would "ride the wave," to add a surfing metaphor here. I'd follow wherever that vein or memory might take me — collecting more pieces to that particular puzzle, that lifetime.

Then eventually, let's say by then I'd collected, analogously, 100 pieces that fit together — maybe that's the equivalent of a whole scene in that past life. Or maybe I'd gathered even 500 pieces that fit together, perhaps what amounts to a whole *series* of scenes in my life. But again, while that may sound like a lot, it's merely 500 pieces out of 100 million in our jigsaw puzzle analogy. So it's a great start, but it's just a small smidgen, a tiny percentage: 0.0005%. That's 5 ten thousandths of one percent — out of one lifetime.

These numbers are not meant to be representative of exact numbers of memories, but merely to give a *perspective* on past lives. It highlights how I may have recalled many different fragments of a lifetime, yet I've still forgotten large swaths of that lifetime. That's the point. My experience is — that's completely normal.

That randomness of my memory recall mirrors exactly what happens with my 21st century memories. So it didn't surprise me at all when that same phenomenon happened with my past life memory recall.

So this "jigsaw puzzle analogy" has been a very helpful teaching tool for me to visualize my memory recall process and to keep it all in a healthy perspective — one that has been realistic and balanced, which has promoted a sense of patience within me. That patience has allowed me to relax with the whole process that's been unfolding for the past almost 50 years now, and to enjoy it. I think that relaxing and enjoying it has also added to my ability to draw insights from these memories and patterns. Being easygoing about when and how the memories have resurfaced, as I've observed them over the years "filling in the jigsaw puzzles," I think has been crucial to allowing me to further educate myself about myself.

For me, that alone is enjoyment enough.

Timeline of Past Lives

—	4000 B.C.	Sumerian businessman
—	3000-1000 B.C.	Egyptian priests (3-4 lives)
—	?	Alien
—	?	Woman
—	800 B.C	Babylonian soldier
—	500 B. C.	Greek orator
—	250 B.C.	Carthaginian slave
—	100 B.C.	Ancient Hebrew
—	1 B.C.-67 A.D.	Simon Peter
—	121-180 A.D.	Marcus Aurelius
—	1157-1199	Richard the Lionheart
—	1200-1700	Tibetan Buddhist monk
		Chinese Buddhist monk
		Son of Muslim leader
		Southeast Asian Buddhist monk
		Japanese samurai
—	1712-1786	Frederick the Great
—	?	Eagle
—	1831-1890	Sitting Bull
—	1918-1943	World War II fighter pilot

About the Author

Kelvin H. Chin is a Life After Life Expert whose past life memories reach back 6,000 years.

He is the Executive Director and Founder of both the Overcoming the Fear of Death Foundation and the nonprofit TurningWithin.org. Working with audiences on death and dying issues since the 1980's, Kelvin has taught numerous seminars worldwide. Bringing greater clarity to his client's thinking in their personal and business life is something Kelvin has applied throughout his 40-year career, including teaching meditation worldwide to more than 5,000 people since the 1970's in schools, businesses, the U.S. Army and at West Point. Kelvin also formerly held CMO roles at AmLaw100 law firms, and was a VP for the American Arbitration Association.

He is the author of "Overcoming the Fear of Death" and "Marcus Aurelius Updated: 21st Century Meditations On Living Life."

Kelvin was born in Boston, raised in Norwood, Massachusetts, and has since lived and worked in 7 countries. He has delivered more than 2,000 presentations with clients in

60 countries. While at Dartmouth College, he studied at the Université de Strasbourg, France. He is a graduate of Dartmouth, Yale Graduate School and Boston College Law School, and is the father of two artistically talented children.

Kelvin can be contacted at
www.KelvinChin.org

and followed on
Twitter @KelvinHChin
Instagram @kelvin.h.chin
Facebook kelvin.chin1

Subscribe to his YouTube channel
youtube.com/c/KelvinChinTurningWithin

Kelvin Chin, 20 months old, Natick, Massachusetts

About the Foundations

The "Turning Within" Meditation and Overcoming the Fear of Death Foundations are nonprofit 501(c)(3) organizations located in Hawthorne, California and are qualified under U.S. federal law by the IRS. Their mission is to help people, regardless of their belief system, reduce their anxiety, and overcome their fear of death and related fears, so they can free up that energy to live more productive, enjoyable lives.

Donations to support the Foundations' work around the world can be made via their websites at:

www.TurningWithin.org
www.OvercomingTheFearOfDeath.org
Donations are tax deductible to the extent allowed by the IRS.

The Foundations also have FaceBook pages at:
www.facebook.com/TurningWithin.org
www.facebook.com/OvercomingTheFearOfDeath

Made in United States
Orlando, FL
22 April 2023

32355986R00150